Biblical Backgrounds
of the
Middle East Conflict

Biblical Backgrounds
of the
Middle East Conflict

Georgia Harkness
Charles F. Kraft

Abingdon
Nashville

BIBLICAL BACKGROUNDS OF THE MIDDLE EAST CONFLICT

Copyright © 1976 by Abingdon

Library of Congress Cataloging in Publication Data
Harkness, Georgia Elma, 1891-1974.
  Biblical backgrounds of the Middle East conflict.
  1. Bible. O. T.—History of Biblical events. 2. Jewish-Arab relations—
History. I. Kraft, Charles Franklin, 1911-   joint author. II. Title.
SB1197.H26 1976   220.9'5   76-22644

ISBN 0-687-03435-3

MANUFACTURED BY THE PARTHENON PRESS AT
NASHVILLE, TENNESSEE, UNITED STATES OF AMERICA

Publisher's Foreword

Georgia Harkness had all her life a great interest in the lands of the Bible and a growing concern for the people of the Middle East. She had often made visits to the Holy Land. She conducted numerous tours giving biblical background lectures to help others understand the depth and sweep of the culture of the Semitic people.

She set out to write this book to help others understand the past as "prologue" to the present and the future. Unfortunately, she was taken ill before she completed her manuscript though she worked on it until the last few days before her death.

Dr. Charles F. Kraft, her one-time colleague at Garrett-Evangelical Theological Seminary, very kindly agreed to complete the writing of the manuscript. We are indebted to him for writing chapters 7 through 10, bringing the story down to the present. The future challenges the good will of all the world's people and lies in the hands of God who created of one blood all peoples of the earth.

Contents

Introduction

It is not news that the conflict between Israel and the Arab states extends back beyond recent encounters. Many informed people know that its roots are earlier than the four wars of 1948, 1956, 1967, and 1973 that have been fought in the Middle East, earlier than the partition of Palestine by the United Nations in 1947, and even earlier than the holocaust that took the lives of six million Jews in the Hitler era.

Occasionally one hears references to conflict in the Middle East that has gone on for generations; but for how many generations, or, in more exact terms, for how many hundreds or thousands of years, is seldom realized. Yet there is historical evidence embedded in the Bible that the conflict has been going on for at least four thousand years, and for reasons that to a very significant degree parallel the forces that are in effect today.

Numerous books are available which cite biblical prophecies, usually out of context, and then draw the conclusion that these are being fulfilled today. To this is usually added the conclusion that the end of the world is imminent, with Christ coming presently in judgment on sinners and to usher in a new heaven and a new earth for the faithful. Let it be said at once that I do not intend to enter into this matter here. I have written my views on the subject in a recent book, *Understanding the Kingdom of*

God. Whatever may be said on biblical eschatology (and variant views are possible on biblical grounds), this is not the concern of the present volume.

Neither am I writing primarily as a propagandist for either side of the Arab-Israeli conflict, though this does not mean that I have no views on the subject. There are elements of political and moral right on both sides. Futhermore, mistakes have been made, and unjustified assaults have been launched from both sides. But this does not mean that we can simply strike an even balance and form no opinion. What is needed is an understanding of the issues and a measure of sympathy for both sides, and this can come best through a knowledge of the backgrounds, both recent and in the remote past, that have produced the conflicts.

One must have deep sympathy with the Israeli yearning for a secure homeland. Both our Christian spiritual kinship with Judaism through the Old Testament, and a knowledge of how the Jews have suffered through the centuries of Diaspora—the Dispersion—lead naturally in this direction. One can understand why our Jewish friends feel hurt if Christians do not fully support their cause. But one must also sympathize with the plight of the Palestinian refugees who feel that their homeland has been taken from them. Until this difficult problem is settled with some measure of justice for both sides, there can be no permanent peace in the Middle East.

Christians who do not fully support the Israeli side of the conflict are often charged with anti-Semitism. Some Christians doubtless deserve this accusation. But there is an important difference between anti-Semitism and anti-Zionism. When Zionism emerged in the early part of this century as the movement of the scattered Jewish people back to the land of their forefathers, there were wide differences of opinion even among leading Jews as to whether this was a practical step. The slaughter of so many Jews in the Nazi concentration camps gave fresh support to the movement, but did not solve the problems connected with it. The problems continue in strife and repeated outbreaks of bloodshed.

Anti-Semitism, like any other form of racism, is unchristian and evil. Yet if one is unable to feel sympathy for the dispossessed Palestinians or to see some justice in their yearning for an independent state on the West Bank of the Jordan, one falls into another kind of anti-Semitism. The Arabs also are Semites—as fully Semitic in their background as are the Hebrew people. One thing I hope to do in this book is to demonstrate that a family quarrel has been going on for many centuries between two groups of Semitic peoples in a small but extremely crucial area of the earth's surface.

This book deals mainly with the past, which should help us to understand the present, and to judge with some measure of probability as to the future. Yet its aim is not to predict what will happen, either eschatologically or politically. I feel sure that any lasting solution of the problems will not come by military force, but by political and diplomatic effort, and that the policy and diplomacy employed must take into account human values and a basic justice for both sides. Anything else will simply lead to an extension of the conflict. What the outcome will be I do not attempt to prophesy.

Why, then, attempt to write this review of the past, including the distant past? The answer is stated graphically in the inscription on the Archives Building in Washington: "The Past Is Prologue." The present conflict in the Middle East is rooted in persistent geographical, economic, cultural, and religious factors which have repeatedly had political consequences and have radically altered the history of that area. The present conflict is the product under modern conditions of centuries of struggle between two great Semitic peoples, each of whom has a great culture and a great spiritual heritage, and has made a great contribution to the civilized world. To see the evidences of this fact is to gain perspective on what is taking place today.

True, history never exactly repeats itself. Changed conditions bring about changes in events. Yet kindred conditions bring about kindred results. In any major social problem, a better general understanding of the complex forces that have brought it into being augurs for a better chance of its effective solution.

The book will begin with a look at biblical geography. In spite of important recent changes in productivity on the surface of the state of Israel, and in economic assets beneath the surface among her neighbors, "the lay of the land" remains nearly as it has always been. On Israel's location hinges much of its strategic and often tragic history. But along with the physical setting we must look at the people: who the Hebrews were and where they came from, who their early neighbors were, what connections developed within and adjacent to Canaan and whether these relations were friendly or hostile—in short, how these neighbors reacted to Israel's presence and Israel to theirs.

This introduction to the land and its people should form the setting for a survey of the whole history of the Hebrew people: the patriarchal period that begins with Abraham, the bondage in Egypt, the Exodus under Moses, the conquest of Canaan, the rule of tribal overlords, and then the establishment of a kingdom, its coming to greatness under King David, the split into two kingdoms after the death of Solomon, the rising strength of enemies to the east and the southwest, the fall of Samaria and later of Jerusalem, the exile in Babylon, the return, and what followed later in subjection to various foreign powers.

In this summary the spiritual factors in biblical history will of course need to appear, for it was a deep commitment to their God and a sense of divine destiny that enabled the Hebrews to survive political conquest and give to the world a lasting heritage. However, the focus of the survey will be the political and social history of the people, and hence the bearing of this past upon the conditions of the present.

The primary concern that has prompted the writing of this book is the hope that bringing these facts to the attention of the general reader who may not be very clearly aware of them may give him a better understanding of the Middle East today. If it could do even a little to promote understanding and thus alleviate intolerance and animosity, this would be reason enough for the undertaking. But I must confess to another quite personal reason. Having served several times as the Bible lecturer for a Bible lands cruise that took us not only to Israel but to the places connected with Paul and the early spread of Christianity, I have come to love this whole area, so rich in history, so crucial to our spiritual heritage. So I have enjoyed writing the book—and I hope that some may enjoy reading it.

1

How the Land Lies

At the outset of a presentation of the convergence of ancient with modern factors in the Middle East conflict, a question of semantics arises. What shall we call this land around which the conflict centers? Even selecting a name by which to speak of it is apt to call forth an emotional reaction from one side or the other.

The religious, and to a considerable degree the popular, name for it in the Western world is "the Holy Land." So it is, with tender ties to three great faiths. But it is by no means holy in the same way to all three. Its holy city, Jerusalem, which means "city of peace," has been fought over more than any other city in the world, and religion is to no small degree a source of the conflict.

The earliest occupants of the country called it Canaan, and we might go back to that. But that was a long time ago. The term *Canaan* seldom appears in the Old Testament after the book of Judges—that is, after the conquest of its former inhabitants—and scarcely at all in the New Testament.

To leap over the centuries to the present, we can, of course, call it Israel. We are on safe ground to refer to "the state of Israel" as a political entity. But just how much of the land belongs to the state of Israel is what the whole conflict is about which has produced four wars within twenty-five years. There is the further problem that when we get back into biblical history, Israel was the name of the northern kingdom which ended with the fall of Samaria to Assyria in 722 B.C., while the southern kingdom, where Jerusalem was located, was called Judah or Judea.

Probably the most neutral designation we can adopt is to call the land by its most familiar name across many centuries: Palestine. But even here we are not out of trouble. *Palestine* is a term derived from the territory of the Philistines, the early and persistent enemies of the Hebrew people, who lived in the area to the southwest now called the Gaza Strip. They were never fully conquered. Herodotus, the Greek "father of history," first gave this name to the area in the fifth century B.C. by referring to it as "the part of Syria which is called Palaistine," and the Roman emperor Hadrian in the second century A.D. made the name official. It has borne it ever since. I have been interested to discover that the references to Palestine in Exodus 15:14; Isaiah 14:29, 31; and Joel 3:4 in the King James Version have been changed to Philistia in the Revised Standard Version and the New English Bible.

So, the common query "What's in a name?" must be answered by saying, "A good deal of history, past and present." What I propose to do is to call the *country* Palestine in deference to long usage, the present *political body* the state of Israel, and the *people* either the Hebrews, the Jews, the Israelis, or, in a corporate sense referring to the past, simply Israel.

1. The Land

Palestine is a very small country. It is about the size of the state of Vermont, and like Vermont roughly rectangular. Its latitude is nearly that of the state of Georgia, with a corresponding climate, though its terrain is so varied that the temperature varies too. The traditional dimension, "from Dan to Beer-sheba," that is, from north to south, is about 150 miles, and with excellent roads it is easily traversed now in half a day. In the south the distance from the Mediterranean to the Dead Sea is barely 50 miles. The country narrows toward the north, and it is only about 25 miles from the important port city of Haifa to the Sea of Galilee.

Yet in spite of the smallness of this land, two things of great importance characterize it. One is that nowhere else in the world have so many battles been fought, so much bloodshed and anguish experienced, over an area of this size and during so many centuries. The other matter is in a brighter vein. Nowhere else has such a little country generated so much faith in God, achieved so much spiritual greatness, or transmitted to the world such an incentive to justice and love in human relations, as have come from this tiny spot on the map of the world.

The Hebrews of the Old Testament considered themselves God's chosen people, linked with their God by a special covenant. In view of all that has been given to the world through their sense of relationship to God, and later through a Galilean Jew on foundations laid by his forefathers, I should not wish to deny that God was directing their destinies. But this was not by easy living—quite the contrary. It was rugged endurance against great obstacles that shaped and deepened the Hebrews' faith and enabled them to survive against great odds. On this basis we can say that the location where God placed them was providential, for this particular location certainly had a great bearing on their total history.

17

This little country of the Jews was tucked in between constraining forces on the west and east. On the west was the Mediterranean Sea, without enough of a harbor along the entire coast to tempt them seaward. Haifa is now an excellent port, and the Crusaders created one at Acre a little to the north of it as Herod the Great had done earlier at Caesarea in the south. In Old Testament times the Hebrews were a landlocked people; their fortunes turned toward the interior.

But where to? On the east lay the vast Arabian Desert. Before the desert there was a strip of fertile land east of the Jordan, and there dwelt the Hebrews' foes the Ammonites, whose name still survives in the name of Amman, the capital city of the Hashemite Kingdom of Jordan. From this stretch of good land, nomadic Arab tribes from the desert who had become semi-agricultural kept pressing in upon the Hebrews, and there were many border conflicts. There was no chance of expansion either eastward or westward.

What of the north and south, however? Here lies the key to Israel's major problems, which bred both disaster and spiritual greatness. This little land was on the direct route—and the only feasible route—between two great civilizations and political forces. In the Tigris-Euphrates valley beyond the desert and somewhat to the northeast were Assyria and Babylonia. To the southwest lay Egypt. Both for commerce and for conquest, the route between the Tigris-Euphrates valley and Egypt lay through the Hebrew territory, for the Arabian Desert was in the way of any shorter route. Nobody dreamed in those times that the desert would prove to be rich in a product much desired by the nations of the world.

Palestine lies at the western end of the long semicircle

of land north of the desert which the great historian Dr. James H. Breasted named "the Fertile Crescent." At the eastern end is Mesopotamia—the land "between the rivers"—which is now called Iraq, and Saudi Arabia and Kuwait are a little further south, near the Persian Gulf. Syria with its ancient capital city of Damascus was, and is, in the central northern section of this area of tillable and traversable land around the desert.

Both Egypt and Babylonia had reached a high state of civilization before the time when the Hebrews settled in Canaan. In his book *The Dawn of Conscience* Dr. Breasted points to Egypt as the place where serious consideration of moral principles first emerged. It is believed that a good many of the practical moral injunctions in the book of Proverbs are adaptations from the Egyptian Wisdom of Amenemopet, and the Book of the Dead has much to say about sin and righteousness as well as about life beyond death. Ikhnaton was a great monotheistic king as early as the fourteenth century B.C., and the Age of the Pyramids considerably antedates Abraham, the largest having been erected about 2900 B.C.

In the Arab East there was a succession of great powers of which Babylon is the most famous. The Code of Hammurabi, formulated there in the twentieth century B.C., shows a remarkably advanced sense of justice in human relations. A great Babylonian commercial civilization was developed, and its caravans went everywhere throughout that section of the world. Every time we look at our timepieces and note the sixty seconds to the minute and sixty minutes to the hour, we are using an inheritance from that area, even as we use arabic numerals in our calculations. If one is prone to think of Arabs as Bedouins from the desert, it is salutary to remember that there was a great Arab civilization long before the ancestors of most of us were anything but unlettered peasants.

But our concern at this point is with the lands of the Bible. This location on the highway of traffic between advanced and powerful peoples kept Israel in touch with the outside world. In a time of peace this could have been a great cultural advantage. It was not a time of peace, however. On the contrary, it was a time of almost continual warfare. Sometimes this was internal strife, but often it was with one or another of these great powers, each of which wished to seize Israel and hold it as a buffer against the other. This is what eventually shattered first the political freedom and then the political existence of Israel and scattered the Jewish people to many lands. In a new setting of technological conditions and changed forms of warfare, but in the same location, the new state of Israel is again contending against her ancient enemies.

2. Some Sectional Variations

It would not be profitable at this point to give a detailed account of biblical geography. More will be said of this as we review the various stages of Israel's history. But at least the general topographical outlines, especially in relation to neighboring peoples, should be understood as a background for this history.

On the western border of Palestine lay the Mediterranean coastal plain. North of Jewish territory was Phoenicia, in what is now Lebanon, with Tyre and Sidon then the principal cities. The narrowness of the land between the Lebanon Mountains and the sea enticed the Phoenicians toward the water and made them great navigators. On the whole, Israel's relations with the

Phoenicians were friendly, much more so than its relations with Syria to the east of Phoenicia. This friendly relationship impinges on Old Testament history in Solomon's dealings with Hiram, king of Tyre, for building materials including timber from the cedars of Lebanon and other imported products. It is reflected still more fatefully in the influence of Jezebel, the Phoenician princess who married King Ahab of Samaria, greatly encouraged Baal worship, and precipitated the attack on the prophet Elijah which led to the famous contest on Mount Carmel, near Haifa, with the prophets of Baal.

In the southern plain, as has been indicated, lay Philistia, now the Gaza Strip, which was controlled by Egypt until the war of 1967. This area has long been a source of uneasiness to the Jews. Its inhabitants were a non-Semitic people who arrived there at about the time that the Hebrews came to Canaan, and established a small but strong state with five principal cities: Gaza, Gath, Ashkelon, Ashdod, and Ekron. Gaza is not only a reminder of the dramatic story of Samson, but it is still there a few miles south of Tel Aviv.

Midway along the coast, west of biblical Samaria and extending from Tel Aviv near ancient Joppa to the Bay of Haifa in the north, lies the beautiful and fertile Plain of Sharon. Along it for many centuries has run a road which the Romans called the Via Maris. But long before Rome arrived on the scene, this was the main route between the great powers of the northeast and of the southwest. Rival armies surged back and forth along it. Along this route marched the hosts of Thutmose III, carrying Egypt's power to the banks of the Euphrates. The Assyrians under Sargon, Sennacherib, and Tiglath-pileser moved the other way along it. Great camel caravans bearing goods for sale

21

traveled along it for centuries, and one of these carried the boy Joseph to Egypt from Dothan, where his brothers were tending their father Jacob's flocks. Today the Plain of Sharon is still a lovely place, dotted with Jewish settlements and kibbutzim that maintain citrus groves, orchards, vineyards, chicken hatcheries, and dairies. And a drive along the Via Maris in sight of the blue Mediterranean is something one does not soon forget.

Turning to the eastern border of Palestine we find a very different setting: the Jordan Valley and the great depression. Geologists believe that this great rift was caused long ago by a volcanic cataclysm, followed by repeated earthquakes. Its sides have been worn down by gradual attrition, except where steep cliffs remain, as in the Golan Heights east of the Sea of Galilee, and on both sides of the Dead Sea.

The Jordan's headwaters are fed by the melting snows of Mount Hermon, the crowning beauty of the Lebanons, nearly two miles high and snow-capped for most of the year. Three streams converge into it. One of these is at Banias, the ancient Caesarea Philippi and the scene of Peter's great confession of Jesus as "the Christ, the Son of the living God." The interplay of history is suggested by the fact that here the Greeks later built a temple to Pan, and by a change of one letter Banias gets its name from Pan.

At the beginning of its course the Jordan flows through a fertile valley flanked by rolling hills. As the northernmost part of Palestine, Jewish settlers have made good use of this. But after a few miles, the Jordan becomes a marsh and modulates into marshy Lake Huleh, four miles long. About a dozen miles to the south of this the river widens to become the Sea of Galilee.

22

Quite apart from its famous history, Galilee is one of the loveliest lakes in the world. No wonder Jesus loved it, called his first disciples along its shores, and after encountering trouble with his Nazareth neighbors after his first sermon, went to live at Capernaum at its northern end. The lake is widest toward the north, nearly eight miles, and thirteen miles long. Harp-shaped, it is called in the Old Testament the Sea of Chinnereth, and its modern Hebrew name is Lake Kinneret, which means harp. In the New Testament it is called not only Galilee but Gennesaret, from the plain on its northwestern shore where it is believed that Jesus spoke the sayings of the Sermon on the Mount. It is also called the Sea of Tiberias, from the capital city erected by the tetrarch Herod Antipas midway along its western shore and named for the Roman emperor Tiberius. Tiberias, now a thriving resort city, is the only one of some ten communities along the shores of the lake which has survived to the present.

The word *Jordan* means "the Descender," and this the river does throughout its course. The Sea of Galilee is already about seven hundred feet below sea level, but the Jordan continues to descend in a muddy, crooked stream to the Dead Sea, which is almost thirteen hundred feet below sea level, the lowest spot on the face of the earth. In the summer when its water is low the Jordan can be forded in some places, but it was not an easy river to cross and has always been a main line of separation between Israel and her Arab neighbors to the east.

The Dead Sea, originally a freshwater lake at the termination of the great rift, for lack of an outlet has long been accumulating salt and other minerals, while many tons of water rise from it in vapor each day. On each side is a narrow barren strip, then steep cliffs. From lofty

23

Mount Nebo in Moab on the eastern side almost all of Palestine can be seen, and there is no exaggeration in Moses' having been shown from it the whole of the Promised Land. To the northwest is Jericho, and a few miles south of it is Qumran, with caves in the cliffs where the Dead Sea Scrolls were found. About two-thirds of the way south on the western side is Masada, famous for its resistance and the self-immolation of its defenders in the struggle with Rome in A.D. 73. Tradition places Sodom and Gomorrah under the waters of the southeastern end, and the Arabs call the Dead Sea the Sea of Lot.

Palestine does not terminate at the Dead Sea. South of it is the Arabah, mainly sand and stones. East of this was ancient Edom, the land of Esau, which contains the remarkable ruins of the red city of Petra. The land rises and then descends again to the Gulf of Aqaba, in recent years a very important outlet to the East for the state of Israel in view of the closing of the Suez Canal.

The land east of the Jordan is part of the biblical world and at times, though not recently, has been considered a part of Palestine. In the north opposite Galilee is the Gaulanitis of the Roman period, now Golan, and the entire northern section as far as the river Yarmuk is the biblical Bashan. South of this is Gilead, an attractive and fertile area, which produced the famous "balm in Gilead." South of that is the high plateau of Moab, and still further south is Edom. This stretch of land faces the desert and has long been in Arab hands. In the days of Greek and Roman conquest it was contended for as a bastion against the desert and what lay beyond it, and has been the scene of many struggles between East and West.

Having looked at both the western and eastern borders of Palestine, we must turn to the central section, the

24

backbone of the biblical world. As is well known, its three main sections were Galilee, Samaria, and Judea. Each has its distinctive features, which even yet have a bearing on the political and cultural scene.

Galilee has a number of high hills or mountains as extensions of the Lebanons, the most famous being round-topped Mount Tabor, which was probably the scene of the Transfiguration, though some scholars place it on Mount Hermon. Galilee is mainly a fertile plateau; Jesus apparently loved its green fields and soft beauty, and made it the scene of many of his parables. It experienced little warfare in Bible times, much less than the sections further south.

Between Galilee and Samaria lies a very important feature, the Plain of Esdraelon, adjacent to the Mount Carmel range which projects southeastward from Haifa. Toward the east it becomes the Plain of Jezreel near Mount Gilboa, and forms a pass between these two mountain barriers. This was the great highway of the nations in the ancient world. From the coast road along the Plain of Sharon, roads branched off here through Galilee to Damascus in the north and through Samaria to the Jordan and the East. Hence, across the Plain of Esdraelon moved not only the caravans but the armies of the ancient world, and many battles were fought upon it. It is no accident that Megiddo in northwest Samaria should have come to be thought of as Armageddon, the scene of the last great battle of mankind.

Samaria in central Palestine was the site of the northern kingdom after the division. Within its borders occurred many events of biblical history. Its ancient capital, also named Samaria, was on a hill six miles northwest of Shechem, an important city of Palestine in its day.

Nothing of the capital city is left today except a sordid little Arab village, but Shechem has become the site of the modern, largely Arab city of Nablus. The greater part of the Palestinian Arabs live in what was once Samaria. By the United Nations partition of 1947 a major section of it was assigned to them, but this was retaken by the state of Israel in the war of 1967. It is a principal bone of contention at present.

South of Samaria is Judea, and here Jerusalem and the surrounding cities of Jericho, Bethlehem, and Hebron are located. It is a high, rocky section, with Jerusalem situated on several hills. Down a steep road leading to Jericho one passes the Wilderness of Judea, the traditional site of the temptations of Jesus. Just south of Bethlehem, verdure ceases for lack of rainfall and the land blends with the Negeb Desert. To the west are lowland hills. Viewed as a whole, the terrain of Judea, save for the height which aided resistance to foes, had little to commend it. Yet here was established the Holy City, revered and fought over for many centuries.

Enough has been said to indicate how the physical location and features of Palestine made probable, if not inevitable, the conflicts which have persisted for centuries and are in the headlines today. No other area is more strategic for the meeting of East and West. In no other area is it more important that the meeting should be one of peace and cooperation instead of strife.

In the next chapter we shall look further at the early inhabitants of the land and at who the Hebrews were. This should enable us to see how these groups became involved with each other in the beginnings of a Semitic family quarrel.

26

2
The
Family Quarrel Begins

The previous chapter attempted to show how the geographical setting made conflict almost inevitable between the Hebrews and their neighbors. The aim of this chapter is to deal with the earliest period of Hebrew history and to indicate the coming together of various Semitic groups in kinship or in rivalry, or, as often occurred, in both combined. This will necessitate looking at both the biblical material and the findings of archaeology, which throw considerable light on the anthropology of the period.

1. The Patriarchal Biblical Narrative

While it is likely that most readers will be familiar with the main points of the biblical story as it is found in the book of Genesis, I shall summarize it since we shall need to refer back to it at a number of points. It is largely a blend of two narratives: the J, or Yahwist, written in the tenth century, and the E, or Elohist, from about two centuries later.[1] They present the memories and traditions of events occurring much earlier, and together make a fascinating story.

Genesis begins with the Creation story of the P, or Priestly, document written in the period of the Exile, but in the second chapter moves into J with a second account

27

of the Creation. There we have Adam and Eve thrown out of Eden for their disobedience to the divine commandment. They become the parents of three sons, Cain, Abel, and Seth. Cain kills Abel, and Seth becomes the transmitter of the human race. After numerous generations and much sinning comes the great flood, when only Noah and his family and the animals he takes with him into the ark are saved. God establishes a covenant with Noah that this will never happen again. Noah's three sons are Shem, Ham, and Japheth, and from these "the whole earth was peopled" (Gen. 9:19). The Semites have long been considered the descendants of Shem, and this is so indicated a little later when the ancestry of Abraham is given (11:10-26). Before this, however, comes the story of the Tower of Babel as an explanation of the confusion of languages and the scattering of peoples over the earth (11:1-9).

Toward the end of chapter 11 the nature of the narrative changes. Up to this point the stories are mythological but spiritually meaningful attempts to account for the creation of the world, the sinfulness and pain of mankind, and the dispersion of the peoples into separate households, lands, and tongues. The remainder of Genesis is patriarchal history, told with great drama.

The story begins as Abraham, with his father Terah, his wife Sarah, and his nephew Lot, sets out from Ur of the Chaldeans in the lower Mesopotamian valley to go to Canaan. But when he came to Haran about six hundred miles to the northwest he stopped for a considerable period. There Terah died, and God gave to Abraham the covenant which was to figure so centrally in later Hebrew history. Many times renewed, its earliest form contains its basic elements and is worth quoting in full:

28

Now the Lord said to Abram, "Go from your country and your kindred and your father's house to the land that I will show you. And I will make of you a great nation, and I will bless you, and make your name great, so that you will be a blessing. I will bless those who bless you, and him who curses you I will curse; and by you all the families of the earth shall bless themselves." (12:1-3)

So the migration began. They entered Canaan, probably from the north through Damascus since Eliezer of Damascus became Abraham's chief steward (15:2). They stopped first at Shechem, then went on south to Bethel and still further south to the Negeb area. After a severe famine had caused a sojourn in Egypt, they returned to southern Canaan and settled at Bethel, which is twelve miles north of Jerusalem. There Abraham and Lot parted company, Lot having chosen the better-watered territory east of the Jordan when given an option. This was to get him into trouble when sinful Sodom and Gomorrah were destroyed (13:8-13; 19:1-29).

Abraham was greatly troubled that he had no heir to fulfill the promise of many descendants who would become a great nation. Then Sarah miraculously bore Isaac in her old age. Her handmaid Hagar had previously borne Abraham a son, Ishmael. Sarah now became so jealous for Isaac that with Abraham's reluctant consent Hagar and Ishmael were driven into the desert, where they would have perished except for divine intervention (15:1–18:15; 21:1-21). A point often overlooked in the story is that God spoke also to Hagar and promised that her son should become the father of a great nation (21:13, 18). To the present, the Arabs claim descent from Abraham through Ishmael, as the Jews through Isaac.

Abraham would have sacrificed his beloved Isaac as a

votive offering to Yahweh on Mount Moriah in Jerusalem had not God stayed his hand (22:1-14). Thus Isaac was permitted to grow to manhood. Desiring that Isaac marry among his own kinsmen rather than take a Canaanite girl, Abraham sent his servant back with rich gifts to Haran in Paddan-aram and brought back Rebekah, the daughter of Bethuel and sister of Laban, to be Isaac's wife (chap. 24).

Isaac and Rebekah had twin sons, Esau and Jacob, Esau being the elder. Through Rebekah's conniving for Jacob, her favorite, in Isaac's old age he was deceived into passing on the family birthright and line of succession to Jacob. This caused enmity between the two brothers, and to prevent Esau from killing Jacob, Rebekah persuaded Isaac to send Jacob back to her brother Laban's home with the hope of marrying one of his daughters (27:1–28:5).

Jacob made the journey and on arriving at Laban's home fell in love with Laban's younger daughter, Rachel, who by modern reckoning was Jacob's first cousin. Having no bride price to offer, he agreed to serve Laban for seven years if he might marry her. At the end of this time, he was tricked into marrying the elder daughter, Leah, and had to serve another seven years for Rachel. They and their two maids, Jacob's concubines, bore him twelve sons, whose names were later to be given to the twelve tribes of Israel (29:1–30:24). The youngest and most loved were Rachel's two sons, Joseph and Benjamin.

Jacob's flocks began to exceed those of Laban, and rivalry developed between them. Jacob decided to take his sizable family and his possessions back to his former home in Canaan. Rachel shrewdly stole and concealed her father's household gods, with which were associated leadership of the family and the claim to the inheritance. This and Jacob's abrupt departure caused Laban great displeasure, but in Gilead they set up a pillar of stones which they called Mizpah and made a covenant not to pass over each other's territory thereafter. From this we have the familiar Mizpah benediction (31:49).

As Jacob and his family moved westward, he wrestled all one night with a messenger of God who told him that his name would henceforth be Israel (32:22-28). As he neared home he was apprehensive of what Esau might do, but there was a joyous reunion and reconciliation. However, Esau decided to take his family and flocks to Edom. "For their possessions were too great for them to dwell together; the land of their sojournings could not support them because of their cattle" (36:7).

The next scene in the drama is the brothers' jealousy of Joseph because of Jacob's favoritism and Joseph's sense of self-importance, and their selling him to an Ishmaelite caravan as it passed through Dothan on its way to Egypt. There Joseph rose to the position of prime minister, next in power to Pharaoh (41:39-45). In a time of famine in Canaan Jacob's entire family migrated to Egypt, where they settled in Goshen just east of the Nile Delta and profited, with the other inhabitants, from Joseph's wise administration. When an Egyptian ruler appeared "who knew not Joseph," this led to the Egyptian bondage and serfdom, the rise of Moses as the leader of Abraham's, Isaac's, and Jacob's descendants, now known as the children of Israel, and the Exodus.

2. The Early Semitic Migrations

In these stories from the tenth century B.C. and somewhat later we see indications of kinship and also of clashes, foreshadowing what was centuries later to become the Arab-Israeli conflict. Abraham and his kinsman Lot parted amicably, but soon the Semites of the valley east of the Jordan were battling those of the west. The descendants of Ishmael and those of Isaac have never felt kindly toward each other. Esau and Jacob, though reconciled, became the forefathers of the Edomites and Israelites, and when Esau married three wives from among the Canaanites, one of them being Basemath the daughter of Ishmael, the stage was set for a reopening of the rift. To look ahead into New Testament times, Herod the Great was an Edomite, and this Arab ancestry was one of the reasons why the Jews hated him.

But let us see what the archaeologists and historians of the early Middle East can tell us. The biblical stories represent the racial memories of the people as they had been told and retold for centuries. They are great literature with a deep religious meaning that is centered in the covenant between Yahweh and his people. We cannot be sure that at every point they are accurate history. Neither should we dismiss them as wholly legendary. There were streams of migration from the lower and then the upper Euphrates valley, and later from Egypt and the Sinai Peninsula, which dovetail with the main outlines of the biblical narrative. We do not need to deny that Abraham, Isaac, Jacob, and Joseph were real persons even though their names may stand for epochs in racial history.

There were numerous early Semitic migrations, and to trace them we must remember the importance of the Arabian Desert and the Fertile Crescent. The desert occupied the vast territory long known as Arabia, and now called Saudi Arabia. It was not all desert sand, for desert grass grew on it and here and there were oases.

32

Nomadic shepherds, like the present Bedouins, could survive on it provided they kept moving their flocks from place to place as the food and water supplies gave out. But the impulse of the more progressive was to move if they could to more fertile territory.

There was fertile land to the east in the Mesopotamian valley, to the north, and over to the northwest, and this became the scene of most of the migrations, including those of the Hebrews. But there was a fertile area also to the south. This lay at the tip of the triangle formed by the Persian Gulf on the east and the Red Sea on the west, now called Yemen. It was then Saba, or Sheba, and later the Romans called it Arabia Felix, or "Arabia the Happy." It was from here that the Queen of Sheba came to visit King Solomon bearing rich gifts of gold, spices, and precious stones (I Kings 10:1-10, 13). She is said to have borne a son by him, named Menelek, who migrated to Ethiopia and there established the dynasty from which King Haile Selassie was a descendant.[2] In any case, there was a Semitic migration from Saba across the Red Sea into Egypt, and thus the Egyptians became a blend of Arabic and African blood.

But the mainstream of migrations from the desert was eastward and northward. At a very early date and certainly before 3000 B.C. the Sumerians had a strong and advanced civilization in the lower Mesopotamian valley, while there were Akkadians to the north. The men of Sumer and Akkad fought each other repeatedly, and after various shifts in power these became the Babylonian and Assyrian empires. Both figure prominently in Old Testament history. It was the Assyrians that conquered Samaria, and the Babylonians, also known as Chaldeans, who took Jerusalem and precipitated the Exile.

To return to the early migrations, Abraham's early home was in Ur of the Chaldeans (Gen. 11:31). This was an important city near what was then the mouth of the Euphrates, in modern Kuwait. Excavations have revealed a great and very ancient city, the capital of Sumer, with substantial defense walls, temples and shrines to the moon god and his consort, and many clay tablets recording extensive business transactions. Just why Abraham and his people left Ur we are not told, but they may have preferred a simpler rural setting.

The journey to Haran, near the headwaters of the Euphrates, was to another important Semitic site. Haran and the neighboring Nahor were in Aram, and this for many centuries was the name for Syria. After the conquest by Alexander the Great, Aramaic became the lingua franca of the entire eastern Mediterranean world, and a Galilean dialect of it was the native tongue of Jesus.

Haran and Nahor, in what the Bible calls Paddan-aram, were both place names and personal names. Laban lived in Nahor, and from there came the wives of both Isaac and Jacob. But according to the biblical genealogy, Haran and Nahor were also brothers of Abraham, Nahor being the grandfather of Rebekah and her brother Laban. Nahor came later to be thought of as the ancestor of the Aramean, or Syrian, peoples, as Abraham of the Israelites.

However legendary the stories may be, their importance to later history is evident. Here the family quarrel appears to have begun, for the Arabs of Syria and the Hebrews of Israel, long bitter enemies, were Semites who originally were thought of as kinsmen who intermarried and mingled their blood in the offspring of Isaac and Jacob.

But these were not the only Semites of those days. A Semitic people who had overrun the entire section and

34

established themselves securely were the Amorites. It was they who brought Babylonia to a high degree of power and also of civilization, and when they migrated, as they did, into both Aram and Canaan, they brought with them elements of Babylonian folklore and culture.

Who were the Canaanites? The archaeologists have found very ancient skeletal remains which lead to the conclusion that there have been people living in Canaan as long as there have been people anywhere. But the immediate predecessors of the Hebrews were the Amorites. They had established themselves as an agricultural rather than nomadic people, with a considerably higher stage of cultural development, before the Hebrews arrived. They brought with them from the Babylon area stories of the Creation, the Garden of Eden, the great flood, and the Tower of Babel, of which there are traces in the biblical stories, though with very different religious overtones.

Another sector of the Canaanites were a branch of the Aramean Semites. Some moved westward from the area that has long been Syria, and established Phoenicia, now Lebanon. As has been noted earlier, they took to the sea, and became purveyors, not only of the trade and commerce but of the civilization of the nations to the east of them. To them we owe our alphabet. Others moved south and southwest to occupy for the most part the lowlands of Canaan while the Amorites held the higher areas.

So the Hebrews found plenty of predecessors when they arrived, Semitic like themselves but with differing backgrounds, and in the conquest of Canaan, which we shall look at in a later chapter, the fight was on. The major non-Semitic people to migrate to this small land were the

Philistines, who occupied the coastal section to the southwest, adjacent to the Negeb and Sinai deserts, now known as the Gaza Strip. The Bible says they came from Caphtor (Amos 9:7). There is no certainty as to where Caphtor was, but this probably means Crete.

The Hittites represent another non-Semitic group with whom the Hebrews mingled and fought. Esau took two of his wives from among the Hittites, and Uriah the Hittite figures prominently in the career of King David (II Sam. 11:2-27). However, the main strength of the Hittites lay to the north in what is now Turkey. Here they established a considerable kingdom which included northern Syria. From this they made occasional forays into Canaan, and the Hebrews regarded them as enemies.

Thus when the Hebrews arrived in Canaan they found a medley of tribes whose names appear often in the Bible in long lists such as "the Hittites, the Amorites, the Perizzites, the Hivites, and the Jebusites" (Exod. 3:17). The specific locations and characteristics of these early occupants of the land need not concern us. To the Hebrews, they all had what the Hebrews desired to possess; to these motley tribes the Hebrews were invaders who had no right to be there. There are different forms of fighting in our day, but the forms of emotional response have not greatly changed.

It seems appropriate to conclude this chapter with a passage from the book of Deuteronomy, probably written in the seventh century B.C. but commonly regarded as the earliest creed in the Judeo-Christian tradition. It refers to Jacob as "a wandering Aramean," which affirms his Syrian ancestry, and goes on to narrate the great events of early Hebrew history through which their God led them by his gracious favor, not only from bondage in Egypt and

36

into the Promised Land, but into nationhood. This may well serve also as an introduction to the next chapter.

A wandering Aramean was my father; and he went down into Egypt and sojourned there, few in number; and there he became a nation, great, mighty, and populous. And the Egyptians treated us harshly, and afflicted us, and laid upon us hard bondage. Then we cried to the Lord the God of our fathers, and the Lord heard our voice, and saw our affliction, our toil, and our oppression; and the Lord brought us out of Egypt with a mighty hand and an outstretched arm, with great terror, with signs and wonders; and he brought us into this place and gave us this land, a land flowing with milk and honey. And behold, now I bring the first of the fruit of the ground, which thou, O Lord, hast given me. (Deut. 26:5-10)

Here we see clearly the early Hebrew longing for a homeland, reinforced by the deep conviction that after great suffering in a land not their own, the Lord had prepared some better thing for them. This longing with a great sense of divine covenant to sustain them in any adversity has given the Jewish people courage and endurance through the centuries. But there were other "wandering Arameans," Syrian kinsmen, who also had a great ambition to possess this land. The inevitable occurred, and it is still occurring.

Notes

1. The first five books of the Bible, called the Pentateuch, with part of the sixth, consist of four main sources woven together to make a connected narrative. These sources, with their anonymous authors, are usually designated by letters. The J. or Yahwist, narrative is so called because the writer's name for God is Yahweh, and the German scholars who first gave it this designation spelled it Jahveh. The Elohist who told the E

story called God Elohim. The D document is mainly our present book of Deuteronomy ("the second law, or law-giving"), and since it was found in 621 B.C. during the reformation and cleansing of the temple under King Josiah, it was probably written shortly before that time. The P, or Priestly, account dates from the Exile in the sixth century, or a little later. These four accounts were woven into one sequence at intervals by unknown editors, or redactors, without regard to the order of their writing. Thus chapter 1 of Genesis is from P; chapter 2 with a second account of the Creation is from J.

2. The biblical record indicates that the Queen of Sheba and King Solomon were much impressed with each other, exchanging rich gifts very freely, but nothing is said of a sexual union.

3

Bondage and
the Birth of a Nation

The previous chapters have dealt almost entirely with the relations between the Hebrew Semites and other Semitic peoples to the north and east of Palestine, now corporately considered to be Arabs. It is evident that conjunctions, including kinship relations, and clashes between these groups appear frequently in the early narratives. We move now to a different scene but one still much involved in the Arab-Israeli conflict—the ancient land of Egypt.

Genetically, the Hebrew people do not stand in as close a relation to the people of Egypt as to those of the Arab states. Yet according to the biblical narrative, there was a mingling of blood. We are told that Joseph married Asenath, the daughter of Potiphera the priest of On, and that she bore him two sons, Ephraim and Manasseh (Gen. 46:20). Both were adopted by their grandfather Jacob in his old age. Manasseh was the elder, and by custom should have received the birthright blessing and inheritance, but with a reversal perhaps reminiscent of Jacob's own receiving of it, he chose to give it to Ephraim (Gen. 48). However, both names were given to the half-tribes that represented the descendants of Jacob through Joseph.

Looking to secular history, we find that Egypt has been so many times occupied by various peoples that there is no pure Egyptian race. Yet politically and religiously, it is affiliated with the Arab world. Arab armies conquered Egypt in A.D. 646, and it has been a Muslim country ever since. Its political control has varied. It was conquered by Alexander the Great in 332 B.C. and became part of the Greek Empire; then for hundreds of years it was ruled by Rome. For the four centuries prior to the twentieth it was ruled by Turkey, save for a brief period when Napoleon conquered it. During most of the first half of the present century it was under British control, and since 1952 it has been an independent republic.

1. Egypt During the Hebrew Bondage

The earliest of all civilizations appears to have begun in Egypt. Five thousand years ago, the Egyptians were erecting huge structures such as the Pyramids and the Sphinx and the great temples at Karnak and Luxor. They were scanning the heavens with telescopes, constructing a calendar from the planetary movements they observed, and writing in a picture language with hieroglyphic (literally "carved by priests") symbols. Mention has already been made of "the dawn of conscience" in Egypt, that is, the giving of serious attention to basic moral principles.

All this was going on long before the Hebrews arrived in Egypt, but we find not one word about it in the Bible. There are several reasons for this. For one, the Hebrews went in as nomads and came out as nomads. They settled on a strip of grazing land in Goshen just east of the Delta, and, except as slaves in Pharaoh's construction business, they had little contact with the people of Egypt. For another, their own culture had not advanced far enough to give them an interest in such intellectual pursuits, and the effort to survive took much of their attention and energy. The principal reason was religious, however. Not only the interest of the people themselves, but certainly the major interest of the later biblical writers who told their story, was centered in the guidance and governing concern of God for his chosen people. This is why the story was told, and except for this central concern we should not have the biblical narratives.

We do learn from the Bible that Egypt in the time of the coming and the going of the Hebrews was governed by pharaohs, apparently with absolute power which could be exercised benevolently or despotically. This is verified by other sources which enable us to place the period of the bondage and Exodus at least approximately in the setting of Egyptian political history. Much has been learned from inscriptions on the buildings, tombs, and statuary of the pharaohs, many of whom apparently wished thus to be immortalized. Another source of great value has been the Tell el-Amarna letters found in Egypt in 1887–88. These are some four hundred clay tablets inscribed in Babylonian cuneiform writing and bearing messages to the pharaohs from Palestinian and other northern governors. They date from about the fourteenth century B.C. and throw light on a relatively advanced culture in Canaan before the Hebrews arrived as well as on the situation in Egypt. Numerous other important discoveries have been made. Enough can be gleaned from such sources outside the Bible to leave no doubt that there was a Hebrew migration to Egypt in the second millennium B.C., a considerable stay in that land, and a departure which resulted in a return to Canaan.

A people called the Hyksos, which means "rulers of foreign lands," invaded and conquered Egypt in the eighteenth century B.C., and though they are not mentioned by name in the Bible it is believed that their fortunes were intertwined with those of the Hebrews. They were a mixed group—Semites, Hittites, and some others. They built up a powerful empire that included not only Egypt but Palestine and Syria, and Shechem became a walled fortress. They moved the capital of their empire from Thebes to the delta area, and from this it seems probable that Joseph's rise to power was under one of the Hyksos pharaohs. They ruled for about a century and a half, during which the Hebrew migration to Egypt probably took place.

Soon after 1600 B.C. an Egyptian revolution broke out which persisted sporadically for some time. In about 1550 B.C. the Hyksos were expelled and their northern territory seized. The militant pharaoh Thutmose III (1501–1447 B.C.), in addition to consolidating Egyptian control over Palestine and Syria, carried his campaign even to the Euphrates. His exploits are sometimes compared to those of Napoleon. Somewhat later, around 1300 B.C., the capital, which had been moved back to Thebes, was again brought to the delta for better control of the Asiatic provinces. It was renamed by Ramses II the "House of Rameses," and simply Rameses or Raamses for short. He reigned from about 1290 to 1224, and a reference in Exodus 2:23 to bondage which followed the death of a king of Egypt seems to fit this period.

Here we find Egyptian and biblical history converging. Ramses II was a great builder, like Herod the Great in a later century, and he had many magnificent buildings, palaces, and tombs constructed, including his own tomb.

This has been unearthed, and I have seen in the museum in Cairo what is said to be his mummy. However that may be, it is stated of the Hebrews in Exodus 1:11 that "they built for Pharaoh store-cities, Pithom and Raamses." It is as certain as anything at that early date can be that Ramses II was the pharaoh of the Exodus.[1]

How long were the Hebrews in Egypt? In Exodus 12:40 it is stated that they dwelt there 430 years. Biblical chronology cannot always be depended on as strictly accurate, but if they entered under a Hyksos pharaoh and left under Ramses II, they were there about four centuries, increasing in numbers from a small group to a large one at the time of the Exodus.

More important than the exact time span, however, was the struggle that was going on during most of this period. There was the internal Egyptian struggle for power which caused repeated changes in control, from the Hyksos rulers in the Fifteenth and Sixteenth Dynasties to Ramses II of the Nineteenth. There was the external struggle between Egypt and the north and east, with these areas under Egyptian control much of the time but with shifts in their governance. And inwardly, there was the struggle between the oppressing pharaohs and the oppressed Hebrews, with the latter long silent for lack of power until God heard their cry and a God-given leader appeared.

In later years the conquest of Palestine was many times attempted, and sometimes successfully. The desire to possess it was natural enough, for as all the great early conquerors knew well, this land was a gateway to the lands that lay beyond it. The Exodus occurred but once. It was ever after to be the most crucial and gratefully remembered event in Hebrew history.

43

2. The Exodus

Repeatedly in the literature of the Old Testament, and especially in the poetry of the Psalms, the deliverance of the Hebrews from bondage by the intervention of their God is celebrated. Even today, faithful Jews commemorate this in the Passover ritual, as did Jesus on the night of his Last Supper. More than any other single element, it has bound Jews together in their centuries of dispersion over the earth.

It is not to discredit this faith or deny God's activity in these meaningful events to say that without the leadership of Moses, the Exodus would not have occurred. God's major mode of action appears to be through human agents, and of these Moses was a very great one. There is no doubt that he was a real person, and a most remarkable man. Some biblical scholars regard the stories of Abraham, Issac, and Jacob as standing for movements rather than individuals, but I know of none who doubts the actual existence of Moses. Who, we may ask, was he?

All that we know of Moses must be gleaned from the biblical narrative. Considering the primacy of a religious rather than a biographical concern in the writers, we cannot expect every element in the story, such as the rod that becomes a serpent (Exod. 4:2-5), to be scientifically accurate. Yet the main outlines are plausible and doubtless on the whole authentic.

We have first the charming story of how the baby Moses was placed in a basket along the riverbank, found by Pharaoh's daughter, and adopted as her son. Its backdrop is not so charming, for such was the enmity of the Egyptian kings toward these unwelcome foreigners that

44

the killing of the male babies to weaken their hold on the land of Goshen may be quite true (Exod. 1:15-22).

As Moses grew to manhood, he appears to have been given all the advantages of living in Pharaoh's court—a preparation for the work he was to do later, though not in the way then expected. Yet as he learned of his Hebrew birth he had a great sense of identity with his own people, and this must have precipitated some inward struggles. The climax came when in anger at seeing an Egyptian beating a Hebrew slave he killed the man. Fearing detection, he fled across the Sinai Peninsula to Midian (Exod. 2:11-15).

Midian was located south of Moab, near the north end of the Gulf of Aqaba. There Moses married. As he was tending the flocks of his father-in-law, Jethro (also called Reuel), to the west near Mount Sinai, he had the vision of the burning bush (Exod. 3:1-6). Whatever its nature, he felt that God was speaking to him and calling him to go back to Egypt and deliver his people. Doubtless his people's woes had occupied his thoughts as he tended his flocks. However that may be, he was now sure of his life's mission and of God's guidance and sustaining power. This was reinforced by God's speaking his own name as I AM WHO I AM, a cryptic term to us, perhaps, but conveying to the early Hebrew mind Yahweh, the Source and Ground of all that is.

Then follows the return of Moses to Pharaoh's court, the hardening of Pharaoh's heart to refuse the release of the people, and Moses' persistence. There is no yielding until after the ten plagues, viewed by the Hebrews as sent by God for their deliverance: water that turned blood-red, frogs, gnats, flies, sickness and death of cattle, boils, hail, locusts, and darkness (Exod. 7:14–12:32). None of these

45

persuaded the ruler to grant release until the tenth—the death of the Egyptian firstborn. Herewith, the Passover ritual was instituted as the messenger of death passed over the homes of the Hebrews and left them unscathed. Its permanence was enjoined in the words, "You shall observe this rite as an ordinance for you and for your sons forever" (Exod. 12:24). Its observance as a sacred rite has continued to the present.

There are two questions about this series of events that the modern mind is apt to raise, though it did not occur to the authors of the J, E, and P narratives, here blended, to raise them. I do so with some hesitation, for readers will certainly not agree as to the answers.

The first is about the matter of miracle. Did God specifically and miraculously send these ten plagues to fall upon the Egyptians while the Hebrews did not experience them? The answer depends at least in part on the meaning of *miracle*, which is now often conceived as the interruption or violation of a natural law. Of this the Hebrews of that era, untutored in natural science, had no conception. To them, Yahweh did everything, sometimes in the great regularities of "seedtime and harvest, cold and heat, summer and winter, day and night," as promised to Noah after the Flood (Gen. 8:22); sometimes in very unusual occurrences. In the basic meaning of *miracle* as "God's wonderful works," something before which to feel amazement and gratitude, the Exodus was a miracle.

But a more difficult question emerges, more germane to the inquiry of this book. How did all this look to the Egyptians? To my knowledge no specific Egyptian description of the plagues and the subsequent exodus of the Hebrews has been found by archaeologists. Some

46

Egyptologists have pointed out that the first nine of the plagues may well have been natural phenomena, caused by unsanitary conditions at the end of the annual inundation of the Nile. But this does not account for the tenth, which must have caused great grief to Egyptian families and is hard to reconcile with the love of God for all people.

It is natural enough that the story should have been written in the light of the Hebrew narrators' gratitude for the God-given deliverance of their people. I should not wish in any way to detract from the sacredness of the Passover rite, as precious to the Jew as the Lord's Supper is to the Christian. By raising the question as to how the Egyptians looked at this series of events if they occurred as recorded, I mean only to suggest that the same event may look glorious or tragic according to the side one stands upon. So it has been through all the centuries in the Middle East conflicts, and so it is today.

3. The Serfs Become a Nation

Where did the Hebrews go when they were delivered by the power of God and the vigorous leadership of Moses? "When Pharaoh let the people go, God did not lead them by way of the land of the Philistines, although that was near" (Exod. 13:17). This would have been along the Mediterranean coast, the main military and caravan highway into Canaan, and to have taken it would have been fatal to the Hebrews' chances of escape. There is some question as to the route they took, but it was probably by way of Lake Timsah, a shallow, marshy body of water just north of the Gulf of Suez; then along the east

47

bank of what is now the Suez Canal and south until they turned inward toward Mount Sinai. The Hebrew words for the water they crossed are *Yam Suph*, "the Sea of Reeds," much more applicable to Lake Timsah than to the Red Sea far to the south. The Septuagint version has perpetuated the mistranslation.

As for the strong east wind that blew back the waters, this has been known to occur. Within the three interwoven strands of the story, we see the miraculous element growing. The first has the parting of the waters as a quite possible natural event; in the second Moses' rod makes the waters part; in the third the waters stand up on each side like a wall. But the main point is the rejoicing in God's providential care. The Song of Miriam, probably contemporary with the event and the oldest bit of poetry in the Old Testament, expresses this joyous praise to Yahweh:

> Sing to the Lord, for he has triumphed gloriously;
> the horse and his rider he has thrown into the sea.
> (Exod. 15:21)

The longer Song of Moses (Exod. 15:1-18) reflects the memory of the event in a later setting, and probably became part of the liturgical cultus.

It is not strange that the Hebrews saw in this event a miraculous deliverance and have continued through the centuries to celebrate it as such. Again it may be pointed out that there is no mention of the grieving wives and children of the Egyptians who perished in the engulfing waters! This could hardly be expected, and since Christians two thousand years later adopt similar attitudes, we had better not blame these ancient Hebrews.

The period in the wilderness, which means the Sinai

48

Peninsula desert, is said to have been forty years, though this is in round numbers rather than exact chronology. It does not connote aimless wandering, but the experience of a nomadic people who must move from place to place to find food and water. Two areas are indicated as stopping-places of considerable duration: Mount Sinai, where the Ten Commandments were given and the covenant renewed; and Kadesh-barnea in the Negeb about fifty miles south of Beer-sheba. It was from the latter that the trek toward Canaan was launched.

The people found life in the desert even more rigorous than slavery in Egypt. Water was scarce, and there was little food even though they were miraculously supplied with sustenance in the form of manna and quails. There was discontent, quarreling, and rebellion against Moses for having brought them there (Exod. 15:22—17:7). He did not have an easy time with them, and it is a clear indication of his greatness that he was able to hold them together at all.

The major event of this period was the giving of the Ten Commandments at the holy mountain and the reestablishing and deepening of the covenant bond with Yahweh. The traditional location of Mount Sinai, or Jebel Musa, is toward the southern end of the Sinai Peninsula, midway between the Gulf of Suez and the Gulf of Aqaba.

The story of the giving of the Ten Commandments is told with great drama in Exodus 19. The commandments follow in Exodus 20:1-17 and are found again with slight variations in Deuteronomy 5:6-21. It has often been said that these emerged from the experience of the people and were codified after they entered Canaan. This may well be true of the Covenant Code of Exodus 20:23—23:33, for it reflects some Babylonian influence. Other scholars, with

49

whom I agree, hold that there is no sufficient reason for doubting the Mosaic authorship of the basic "ten words," though they acquired accretions later.[2] We are told that on the advice of his father-in-law, Jethro, Moses established a system of law courts to judge the people, he himself retaining the hard cases (Exod. 18:26). But the main evidence in addition to the biblical narrative lies deeper. A leader who could take a band of rebellious former slaves and transform them into a united people with a sense of their national destiny was certainly capable of being a great lawgiver under divine direction. And that it was under God's direction is evidenced, furthermore, by the fact that Moses took a group of miscellaneous clans, supposedly of common origin but impregnated with Egyptian ideas of worship, and united them about the worship of one God—their God—in a lasting covenant.

It was this covenant, reaffirming divine protection but also laying down the essential condition of obedience, that brought the people together and gave them a sense of their potential greatness as a holy nation. It reads:

Thus you shall say to the house of Jacob, and tell the people of Israel: You have seen what I did to the Egyptians, and how I bore you on eagles' wings and brought you to myself. Now therefore, if you will obey my voice and keep my covenant, you shall be my own possession among all peoples; for all the earth is mine, and you shall be to me a kingdom of priests and a holy nation. (Exod. 19:3-6)

Obviously, the people did not always keep their side of the covenant. Even before the story of the giving of the Ten Commandments graven on two tablets is finished, we read of how they were turning under Aaron's leadership to making a golden calf and worshiping the gods of Egypt (Exod. 32:1-6). God was angry and so was Moses, but both

50

relented and the covenant was renewed. However often violated, it has remained a guiding light of the Hebrew people through many centuries both of nationhood and of exile.

But if their destiny was to be fulfilled, they must move forward into the Promised Land. How they did this, and what befell them there, must be our inquiry in the next chapter.

Notes

1. In this survey of the interplay of Egyptian with Hebrew history I have for the most part followed the accounts given in Bernhard Anderson, *Understanding the Old Testament* (Englewood Cliffs, N.J.: Prentice-Hall, 1957), and Elmer W. K. Mould, *Essentials of Bible History*, rev. ed. (New York: Ronald Press, 1951). They are in substantial agreement except for some deviations as to dates. Mould, p. 99, regards Ramses II's son Merneptah as the pharaoh of the Exodus, thus placing the wilderness experience and the entrance into Canaan about a generation later. Anderson follows the usual, and I believe more plausible, assumption that the contest leading to the release of the Hebrews was between Moses and Ramses II.

   While I am by nature inclined to be incredulous when relics are shown me, there is enough possibility that the embalmed body taken from the tomb of Ramses II may really be that of Moses' contemporary and adversary to give one a curious sense of the transiency of time.

2. In my earlier biblical instruction it seemed to be taken for granted that the Decalogue emerged from the experience of the people, divinely guided but with no single author. As today in numerous passages archaeology seems to affirm rather than deny what the Bible states, there seems to be a trend toward the Mosaic authorship of the Decalogue (cf. Anderson, pp. 55-59). In either case, such basic and universal moral principles bespeak their divine origin.

51

4

On to
the Promised Land

A large part of the Pentateuch (the first five books of the Old Testament) seems to indicate Mount Sinai as a base for the time in the wilderness. But on examination we find that the latter part of Exodus, all of Leviticus, and the first ten chapters of Numbers consist almost wholly of religious rites and social provisions to govern the life of the covenant people. These probably accumulated over a considerable period and were brought together much later by the J, E, and P writers.

In Numbers 10:11 we are told that "in the second year, in the second month, on the twentieth day of the month," the guiding cloud that had brought the Hebrews to the wilderness of Sinai was lifted, and brought them by stages to the wilderness of Paran. This was to the northeast, near the head of the Gulf of Aqaba, and still further north was the Wilderness of Zin, where Kadesh-barnea (or Kadesh) was located. It was apparently here that the Hebrews made their main base during the generation or so that elapsed after the Exodus. In any case, it was from this point that they attempted to enter Canaan. This was no easy matter, as we shall note presently, and in the process the Semitic family quarrel was strongly accentuated.

1. Barriers Emerge

Before tracing the opposition from without, let us note that from within. The covenant had vivid reminders, as in the "tent of meeting" where Moses talked face to face with God (Exod. 33:9-11), in the ark that contained the two graven tablets of the law and was carried wherever the people went, and in the ritualistic observances. But these were apparently not enough to keep the people happy and united. There is a clear picture of their unrest in these words:

> Now the rabble that was among them had a strong craving; and the people of Israel also wept again, and said, "O that we had meat to eat! We remember the fish we ate in Egypt for nothing, the cucumbers, the melons, the leeks, the onions, and the garlic; but now our strength is dried up, and there is nothing at all but this manna to look at." (Num. 11:4-6)

Furthermore, there was rebellion against Moses' authority. Even Miriam and Aaron, his sister and brother, grumbled about him, jealous that the Lord spoke more directly through him than through them. Korah led a rebellion of 250 prominent leaders of the congregation against Moses and Aaron, and said to them, as more than one lay group has said in later years to their leaders, "You have gone too far!" (Num. 16:1-3). It is said of Moses that he was "very meek, more than all men that were on the face of the earth" (Num. 12:3). But he was far from spineless, and the way he handled these incidents makes interesting reading.

It may be that such evidences of discontent led Moses under God's direction to feel that the moment had come to push toward Canaan. Spies were sent northward who brought back samples of the fine fruit of the land and a glowing report of a land flowing with milk and honey. Yet not wholly so. There was a note of caution.

Yet the people who dwell in the land are strong, and the cities are fortified and very large; and besides, we saw the descendants of Anak [an aboriginal giant] there. The Amalekites dwell in the land of the Negeb; the Hittites, the Jebusites, and the Amorites dwell in the hill country; and the Canaanites dwell by the sea, and along the Jordan. (Num. 13:28-29)

This caused a great commotion among the people, afraid to go lest they be slain, unwilling to stay where they were under Moses' leadership, eager to choose a captain who would take them back to Egypt (Num. 14:1-4). It was no small crisis in Moses' leadership! He felt it to be God's will that they should not attempt an entrance to Canaan from that angle, but some hotheads went, and were ignominiously defeated (Num. 14:39-45).

It should be noted at this point that the report of the spies accords very well with what is known from other sources as to southern Canaan and its pre-Hebrew Semitic occupants. The hill country of the Jebusites, later Jerusalem, was easy for its occupants to defend, very difficult to take. The Amalekites, believed to be descendants of Esau's grandson Amalek (Gen. 36:12, 16), were nomadic marauders who lived in the desert south of Canaan, directly between where the Hebrews were and where they wanted to be. Both by blood feud and by location they were chronic enemies of the Hebrews. The Hittites who had come earlier from Asia Minor were still around. The Amorites were the principal pre-Hebrew settlers of Canaan, and they occupied the highlands. With a Babylonian background they were distant relatives but not friends of the Hebrews. Both Yahweh and Moses knew that there must be a better way to enter Canaan.

54

So there was, though not an easy one. The chronology is unclear as to what time intervened before the Hebrews broke camp from Kadesh, but apparently it was a considerable period. Then approaches were made to the king of Edom for permission to pass through his territory by the King's Highway, a main route which led from the copper mines near the head of the Gulf of Aqaba north to Damascus. The Hebrews promised not to deviate from the road to the right or the left and to pay for any water they might use, but the suspicious king gave a peremptory refusal (Num. 20:14-21). So the only thing to do was to go north along the western border of Edom, then east and north to encircle Moab. They seem to have had no serious trouble at first. But when they came to the territory of Sihon king of the Amorites and Og king of Bashan, they were opposed, but decisively defeated their opponents; then Balak the king of Moab became very uneasy. Thereupon follows the story of the summoning of Balaam, a Syrian diviner, to pronounce a curse on the Israelites, of his talking ass that resented being struck by her master, and of the angel of the Lord that intervened to prompt Balaam to utter a blessing on Israel instead of a curse (Num. 22:2–24:25).

To the modern mind this may seem like an interesting bit of folklore. But to the narrators of the story, which occupies three chapters, it was sure evidence that the blessing of the Lord was upon the people of Israel. The setting is told in a single sentence: "Then the people of Israel set out, and encamped in the plains of Moab beyond the Jordan at Jericho" (Num. 22:1). This means that they settled for a time in Transjordan opposite Jericho, with the crossing of the Jordan and the conquest of Jericho and Canaan coming later after the death of Moses. The rest of

55

the book of Numbers is devoted mainly to the numbering of the people; to the listing of many places not mentioned elsewhere, said to be taken from Moses' journal; and to ritualistic matters. The principal historical items are a victorious war on Midian for having joined Moab in opposing the Israelites, and the designation of Joshua as successor to the now aging Moses.

These people with whom the Israelites had to contend before reaching a vantage point for entering Canaan were all related to them in one way or another. I have already commented on the Amalekites and others who stood in the way of their entry from the south. As for their entry from the east, it may be helpful to recall some things said in earlier chapters of this book.

Edom was Esau country, with a mingling also of the Ishmaelite strain through Esau's marriage to Ishmael's daughter. It was already thoroughly Arab without having yet assumed this name.

Moab was the land Lot had chosen when he parted from his uncle Abraham so that each might have more room for his flocks, and his descendants still lived there. On the whole, Moab was more friendly to the Hebrews than any other of these peoples east of the Jordan. We have in a later setting the beautiful story of Ruth the Moabitess, who came to Bethlehem out of fidelity to her mother-in-law, Naomi, married their kinsman Boaz, and thus became the great-grandmother of David and an ancestor of Jesus. Yet when the Israelites in great numbers moved northward along Moab's eastern border and settled down in Moab territory just north of the Dead Sea, it is not surprising that the king of Moab did not like it! Balak wanted some help to dislodge them, whether by way of a Syrian soothsayer or of military aid from Midian to the south. There is a graphic picture in his words to the elders of Midian: "This horde will now lick up all that is round about us, as the ox licks up the grass of the field" (Num. 22:4).

As for Midian, this was the land to which Moses had fled for succor in his youth when he slew the Egyptian foreman; there he had had the vision of the burning bush and heard Yahweh calling him to his life's work; there he had married his wife, Zipporah; from there his father-in-law, Jethro, had come to help him establish a legal system by which to deal with his unruly people. One can imagine that Moses, and Zipporah too if she was still living, must have had mixed emotions as he felt God was calling him to muster an army to take vengeance on the Midianites. The story as it is told in Numbers 31 sounds vitriolic even for that day, with no trace of compassion for the defeated Midianites. Compunction in the matter of killing women and babies, burning cities and encampments, and seizing enormous amounts of booty is not indicated, for war then as now bypassed moral considerations.

Regarding the kingdoms of Sihon and Og, north of Moab, it is not clear whether the Hebrew people as a whole moved into the territories and then returned to Moab, or whether only an armed contingent confronted and defeated these rulers.

What is clear is that all these people lived along the arable strip between the Jordan and the Arabian Desert. They were Semites whose ancestors, like those of the Hebrews, had sought a home in fertile territory. To them the Hebrews were invaders; to the Hebrews they stood in the way of a God-given destiny. This confrontation came early in the Arab-Israel conflict, but the battles there fought were not to be the last.

We do not know how long the main body of the

Hebrews stayed on the plains of Moab. But it was long enough for the tribes of Reuben, Gad, and half of Manasseh to decide to stay there in the section that had been taken from Sihon and Og, which came to be called Gilead. We are told that Moses gave them this territory on condition that they would help their fellow Hebrews conquer Canaan—a condition which they accepted (Num. 32:28-33).

2. The Crossing

The word Hebrew comes indirectly from the verb 'abar, which means "to cross over." The Hebrews and their Sumerian predecessors the Habiri, or Habiru, were boundary crossers. We come now to the most important crossing of all their history.

As we move from the book of Numbers to Deuteronomy, we find a new style of writing. Up to this point the sequence of history has been stated in a blend of the J (Yahwist) document from the time of the United Kingdom in the tenth century B.C., the E (Elohist) from the eighth century, and the P (priestly) from the time of the Exile or a little later. The D document, for Deuteronomy, which means "the second giving of the law," was found in the renovation of the temple under King Josiah in 621 B.C. and was probably written shortly before that time. Besides legal and ritualistic matter it contains a long discourse attributed to Moses as a farewell address and with it a beautiful poem or hymn called the Song of Moses.

Deuteronomy, like the material previously discussed, was written long after the time of Moses, but preserved some great religious and racial memories. In it Moses reviews the previous great events of Israel's history: the Exodus, the making of the covenant, the period in the wilderness, the victories east of the Jordan. Its purpose is to call upon the Hebrews to remember gratefully all that Yahweh has done for them and in return to be faithful to their side of the covenant. Victory, prosperity, and all good things are promised to the faithful; the opposite fate awaits those who forsake the Lord and disobey the obligations of his covenant.

In the last chapter of Deuteronomy, Moses goes up to the summit of Mount Nebo, opposite Jericho, and surveys all the land which the Lord has promised to his people. It stretches from Gilead and Dan in the north to the "western sea" (Mediterranean), and to the land of Judah and the Negeb in the south. (It is quite possible to see all this from that elevation, so small is the land of Israel.) Then the Lord says to Moses: "This is the land of which I swore to Abraham, to Isaac, and to Jacob, 'I will give it to your descendants.' I have let you see it with your eyes, but you shall not go over there" (Deut. 34:4).

So Moses died, and Joshua the son of Nun took the reins of leadership in his stead. A great life—not a perfect life, for it had human limitations, but a truly great life—had finished its earthly course. The constructive achievements of this servant of God in pointing men toward God, in setting forth God's moral demands, and in leading and sustaining the people during the birth throes of a nation—these are contributions to the world which persist to the present day.

The account of the crossing of the Jordan into the Promised Land is given in Joshua, chapters 1 through 6, and in the next six chapters we find an account of what appears to be a quick subjugation of the rest of Canaan.

Joshua 1–12 is a dramatic story in the Deuteronomic vein of complete success for God's faithful people, and complete disaster for the people of Canaan who stood in their way. However, the first chapter of the book of Judges indicates a much more gradual conquest and is probably historically the more reliable.

How did this large company of people manage to get across the Jordan? There is the miraculous account of the waters standing up in a heap as soon as the priests bearing the ark of the covenant reached the river's brink, remaining in this state until all had passed safely over (Josh. 3:11-17). If one prefers a more natural explanation, there are fords at various places in the Jordan, including one near Jericho which is referred to in connection with the men looking for the Hebrew spies who were being concealed by Rahab the harlot (Josh. 2:7). Some say there was a landslide, not uncommon along that geological fault. One may take his choice.

Why was the capture of Jericho so important? It was essential that it be seized first, not only because it was the nearest city, but because it was the gateway to the rest of Canaan. Through it ran three roads, northwest into central Palestine, west up a long, steep slope into Jerusalem, and southwest to the plateau of Judea. Nothing is said of Jericho's beauty, but it stood on an extensive oasis amid barren desert and wilderness, and its location enables it to be a lovely city even today after various rebuildings.

3. The Conquest

It would not be fruitful to try to trace here all the many place-names and the many names of kings of the little city-states conquered by the Hebrews. The kings are usually reported as conquered and slain, often with a gory and gruesome destruction of all their people. I shall try only to indicate the probable historical setting.

First, when did this invasion occur? Probably during the latter half of the thirteenth century B.C., between 1250 and 1200. This fits the timing of the reign of Pharaoh Ramses II (ca. 1290–1224 B.C.), allowing forty years or at least a generation for the time spent in the Sinai Peninsula and east of the Jordan. Various scholars estimate it to have occurred a little earlier or later, but this is a safe approximation.

By tracing the medley of cities which the biblical account says were attacked and conquered, some outlines become clear. With Jericho conquered and everybody and nearly everything in it destroyed (Josh. 6:21-25), Rahab and her family alone being spared because she had hidden the spies, the Hebrews seem to have conducted campaigns in three directions. They first moved into the central highlands, taking Ai, which probably means Bethel, on the way. They then moved south into the hill country, wisely avoiding Jerusalem, taking several cities and making an alliance with Gibeon. It was here that the sun stood still for a day, and the moon over the valley of Aijalon, or so we are told on the authority of the lost Book of Jashar (Josh. 10:12-14). The third thrust was to the north, beyond the valley of Jezreel and into what was later to be called Galilee.

The main objectives were the high areas. For this there were both economic and military reasons. The high places with their rough and broken terrain were suitable for grazing but not for agriculture. The Canaanites with their more advanced economic development had already be-

61

come farmers and had occupied the plains, while the Hebrews were still nomads or seminomadic shepherds. Furthermore, the Canaanites had iron chariots and heavy armor. These were very effective on level ground but an encumbrance in the mountains, and the Hebrews shrewdly preferred to fight by sudden attack or ambush in these areas.

Whether the Hebrews came into control of the land quickly or gradually, they unquestionably took possession of strategic parts of it. This process was hastened by feuds among the many Canaanite princes who are referred to as kings, and along the coastal plain by incursions into Canaan by the Philistines, who later were to become enemies of the Hebrews. But the main reason for the Hebrew successes goes deeper.

At every turn, the Hebrews believed that their God gave them the victory. This is a tendency of long standing which among them took on special meaning and gave them superior force. Surveying the scene either from the viewpoint of the Hebrew prophets or from the insights of Christianity, it is hard to square events like the following, typical of many which are recorded, with the will of a gracious or a just God: "Then Joshua went up with all Israel from Eglon to Hebron; and they assaulted it, and took it, and smote it with the edge of the sword, and its king and its towns, and every person in it; he left none remaining, as he had done to Eglon, and utterly destroyed it with every person in it" (Josh. 10:36-37).

Apparently there was no thought of comparing the "Thou shalt not kill" of the Mosaic law with the exigencies of conquest. Unfortunately, this has occurred in many lands and in many conflicts since that time.

Yet in a deep sense it was their faith that gave the

Hebrews the victory, for they had a conviction that united them and enabled them to fight with a zeal that was overwhelming. The Canaanites had their Baal worship, but nothing comparable in power. Tinctured with fury though it was, the Hebrews' understanding of their relation to their God had an affirmative side that must not be lost from our Judeo-Christian heritage. Perhaps it has nowhere been better stated than in God's words to Joshua at the beginning of the enterprise: "Have I not commanded you? Be strong and of good courage; be not frightened, neither be dismayed; for the Lord your God is with you wherever you go" (Josh. 1:9).

5

The
Conflicts Continue

The Hebrews were now in Canaan, but by no means in full possession of the Promised Land. As I indicated in the previous chapter, the first twelve chapters of Joshua recount one victory after another, as if the conquest were quick and complete, and so ruthless that one would think hardly any Canaanites were left alive. The next several chapters of Joshua deal mainly with the division of the land among the twelve tribes. But the book of Judges gives quite a different picture. Its first sentence reads, "After the death of Joshua the people of Israel inquired of the Lord, 'Who shall go up first for us against the Canaanites, to fight against them?'" The greater part of Judges and of I Samuel is an account of various battles to possess the land.

Three enemies remained to be overcome. The first was the resident Canaanites, who still held much of the more fertile agricultural land. The second was the Amorites of the territory east of the Jordan. Both of these were Semitic kinsmen of the Hebrews, however hostile and distantly related. The third, who made much trouble for a long time, was a new non-Semitic enemy from the southwest coastal area, the Philistines.

1. The Tribal Confederacy[1]

Before leaving the book of Joshua, we need to look at its very important ending, and what it shows of the tie that gave the Hebrews a sense of unity in spite of much diversity. We are not to suppose that the twelve tribes always dwelt peacefully with one another. In even so small a territory there were geographical disputes and counterclaims that caused divisions, and the leaders did not always agree. But the one thing that held them together was their common relationship to Yahweh, their covenanted God. Upon occasion this could rally them to unite to avenge a wrong or defeat a common enemy.

The last two chapters of the book of Joshua give strong evidence of this unity. Each gives an account of a great assembly from all the tribes, of "the elders, the heads, the judges, and the officers of Israel" (24:1). These were probably two different assemblies, that in chapter 23 being Joshua's farewell address in his old age, that in chapter 24 possibly earlier and centering directly in the renewal of the covenant. In Joshua's address he pays a moving tribute to the way in which the Lord their God has led them. God has given victory to Israel. He will continue to do so if they are faithful to him and to his law. But if they begin to serve other gods, God's favor will be withdrawn. "Then the anger of the Lord will be kindled against you, and you shall perish quickly from off the good land which he has given to you" (23:16).

The assembly recorded in chapter 24 is historically the more important. It was convened at Shechem, between Mount Ebal and Mount Gerizim. (Present-day tourists may locate this site from its proximity to Jacob's well.) Why Shechem? It was a vital spot in Israel's inheritance. It was the family home of Jacob, and Joseph was buried there, his bones having been carried back to the family plot through all the wilderness journey (Josh. 24:32). Apparently Hebrews were still living there whose ancestors did not migrate to Egypt, for there is no mention of any battle for the conquest of Shechem. The Hebrews there may have become amalgamated in varying degrees with their Canaanite neighbors, and needed to be reminded that Yahweh was also their God.

The significance of the assembly was the renewal of the covenant, given long before to Abraham and then to Moses. Joshua opens the assembly with the words, "Thus says the Lord, the God of Israel . . ." Then follows an extended historical summary in which God speaks of his dealings with Israel from the time of Terah and Abraham beyond the Euphrates through the migration to Canaan, the bondage in Egypt, the Exodus, the time in the wilderness, the contest with the Amorites beyond the Jordan, the crossing, the conquest, and his gift to them of a land on which they had not labored and cities which they had not built.

Then follows the crux of the covenant—the terms on which Yahweh will still be their God:

Now therefore fear the Lord, and serve him in sincerity and in faithfulness; put away the gods which your fathers served beyond the River, and in Egypt, and serve the Lord. And if you be unwilling to serve the Lord, choose this day whom you will serve, whether the gods your fathers served in the region beyond the River, or the gods of the Amorites in whose land you dwell; but as for me and my house, we will serve the Lord. (24:14-15)

Warned that Yahweh is "a holy God, a jealous God" who would not forgive their serving foreign gods, the people took vows of allegiance. The covenant was sealed by setting up a memorial stone beneath the oak in the sanctuary of the Lord.

Thus, Joshua 24 marks an important step in Israel's history. The covenant did not originate at this assembly, but its renewal and the solemn vow taken in response to the challenge "Choose this day whom you will serve" cemented the Hebrews together as nothing else could have done.

2. The Period of the Judges

Joshua was a very effective leader and general under whom the early stages in the conquest of Canaan occurred, which included the seizure of most of the hill country with the exception of Jerusalem. For nearly two centuries, from about 1200 to almost 1000 B.C., he was succeeded by local chieftains known as judges. They were not primarily legal figures in the modern sense, though they were sometimes called upon to settle disputes, but rather warlords and chief administrators of a tribe or group of tribes. They did not come to power by hereditary kingship, but by their "charisma." This word is not in the Bible, but it has a double meaning, and one of these is very biblical: they were filled with the Spirit of God, and hence called of God to rule over the people. The judges were also charismatic in the more modern sense of possessing personal qualities by which they convinced the people to accept their leadership.

In this brief survey it will be impossible to deal with all the judges or with what the Bible recounts of their exploits. I shall, however, select some incidents which were both important to Israel's history and illustrative of the ongoing conflict between Israel and her Semitic kinsmen, now neighbors who had become enemies.

Let us begin with the most strategic area still held by the Canaanites after Joshua's conquests. This was the Plain of Esdraelon between Galilee and Samaria, merging in the east into the Valley of Jezreel. In the Bible it is all called Jezreel. As was noted earlier, this was a very important area in Hebrew history. Through it ran the main route from Egypt into Damascus to the north and Mesopotamia to the east, and whoever held this could control both commercial and military expeditions. At the pass between the mountains at the southwestern end of the plain was the Canaanite fortress of Megiddo, scene of many battles through the centuries and the predicted Armageddon of the last great battle of mankind (Rev. 16:16).

Israel must possess this area. But how? The answer came through the remarkable woman judge Deborah. With Barak to command her military forces, she undertook the venture. In the account of how she outlined to him her plan of action, a sentence appears which I have seldom seen dwelt upon: "Barak said to her, 'If you will go with me, I will go; but if you will not go with me, I will not go'" (Judg. 4:8). She agreed to go, and rallied to their assistance five of the Israelite tribes. With their help and that of a heavy rainstorm which caused the banks of the river Kishon to overflow and mired the heavy Canaanite chariots, the victory was won.

The story is told in prose in Judges 4 and more eloquently in an early and probably contemporary poem in Judges 5. One feels in this poem the power of Deborah, who "arose as a mother in Israel"; her praise for the loyalty of the tribes of Ephraim, Benjamin, Zebulun,

Issachar, and Naphtali who responded to the call; and a stinging rebuke of Reuben, Dan, Asher, and the dwellers in Gilead who took no part in this great battle of independence. One hears the rhythm of galloping hoof-beats, sees the inglorious death of Sisera at the hands of Jael the Kenite, and feels with Sisera's mother her sorrow as she watches in vain for his return. It is one of the great pieces of Hebrew literature.

Turning eastward, we find the people of Israel still in trouble from the other side of the Jordan. Eglon the king of Moab gathered about him the Ammonites and Amalekites of that area, defeated Israel, and repossessed Jericho, "the city of palms" (Judg. 3:13). We are told that this situation lasted for eighteen years (3:14). It is unclear how far the overlordship of Moab over Israel extended west of the Jordan, but apparently it was for a considerable distance. Then the Lord raised up Ehud, a Benjaminite, as Israel's deliverer. The story is told in considerable detail in Judges 3:15-30. Ehud carried tribute to Eglon, but also a concealed two-edged sword which he plunged into Eglon's fat belly as soon as they were alone.[2] This and the seizure of the fords of the Jordan against the Moabites precipitated a battle in which ten thousand of them were killed, and Israel again possessed the land. Needless to say, had the Moabites been telling the story they might not have been so sure it was the Lord's doing.

The two points of view become still more evident a little later during serious trouble with the Ammonites in Gilead, which each side claimed by right of possession. After a considerable amount of conflict, the people of Israel were told by Yahweh that trouble had come upon them because they had served foreign gods. They agreed to renounce them, and Jephthah of Gilead became their

leader. A few citations from the story, which is told at
length in Judges 10:6–12:7, must suffice.

> Then Jephthah sent messengers to the king of the Ammonites
> and said, "What have you against me, that you have come to me
> to fight against my land?" And the king of the Ammonites
> answered the messengers of Jephthah, "Because Israel on
> coming from Egypt took away my land, from the Arnon to the
> Jabbok and to the Jordan; now therefore restore it peaceably."
> (Judg. 11:12-13)

Thereupon Jephthah recounts at length the history of
Israel as it is related to the territory east of the Jordan, and
speaks what seems to him the decisive word: "Will you
not possess what Chemosh your god gives you to possess?
And all that the Lord our God has dispossessed before us,
we will possess" (11:24).[3] To him that seemed to clinch
the matter. But not to the other side! "But the king of the
Ammonites did not heed the message of Jephthah which
he sent to him" (11:28).

The upshot of the matter was Jephthah's vow to offer as
a burnt offering to the Lord the first person who met him
on his return if he could have victory in battle. The victory
was won, and the account ends with the moving story of
how his own daughter was the first to meet him and hence
to become the offering (11:29-40).

Still another source of trouble which illustrates Israel's
conflict with her Semitic neighbors to the east, but at the
same time somewhat of a drawing together with the
Canaanites, lay in the Midianite raiders who came in on
camels from the Arabian Desert. They seized and destroyed the animals and crops of both the Israelites and
the Canaanites.

For whenever the Israelites put in seed the Midianites and the Amalekites and the people of the East would come up and attack them; they would encamp against them and destroy the produce of the land, as far as the neighborhood of Gaza, and leave no sustenance in Israel, and no sheep or ox or ass. For they would come up with their cattle and their tents, coming like locusts for number; both they and their camels could not be counted; so that they wasted the land as they came in. And Israel was brought very low because of Midian; and the people of Israel cried for help to the Lord. (Judg. 6:3-6)

The answer was Gideon to the rescue, acting partly in blood revenge because the Midianites had slain his brothers (Judg. 8:18-21). Gideon destroyed the altar of Baal which his own father had erected, and replaced it with an altar to Yahweh. Summoning help from neighboring tribes, he raised an army and drove back the defeated Midianites (Judg. 6:11–8:12). The people wished to make him a king, but he declined. This incident shows not only a growing convergence of the fortunes of the people, but also how deeply Canaanite worship had infiltrated Israel, for as soon as Gideon died, "the people of Israel turned again and played the harlot after the Baals, and made Baal-berith their god" (Judg. 8:33).

The story does not end here. Gideon had many wives from among the Hebrews, who bore him seventy sons, and a Canaanite concubine in Shechem. She and Gideon had a son named Abimelech. After Gideon's death Abimelech killed all but one of his brothers, and on the basis of his Shechem kinship demanded that he be made king. This was a practice of the Canaanites but not of the Hebrews, whose only king was Yahweh. Abimelech succeeded in reigning over Shechem for three years, which ended in his death and in the destruction of the city (Judg. 9).

This episode indicates that the tribal confederacy was

71

weakening. Another incident with which the book of Judges ends is a gruesome story (chaps. 19–21) which can be cited as evidence of either the strength or weakness of the confederacy. A certain Levite living in Ephraim had a concubine from Bethlehem. After a visit to her father's home they stopped overnight in Gibeah among the Benjaminites. There some rascals of the city raped and abused the girl all night until in the morning she was dead. The Levite cut the corpse of his concubine into twelve pieces and sent them throughout all Israel to rally the people to take revenge on Gibeah. This led to a savage war between Benjamin and the other tribes which almost exterminated the Benjaminites. But while none of the other tribes would permit their daughters to marry into the tribe of Benjamin, they allowed the Benjaminites to lie in wait and seize the daughters of Shiloh as they came out to dance at a religious festival. This inglorious tale gives credence to the words with which the book of Judges ends: "In those days there was no king in Israel; every man did what was right in his own eyes."

3. Another Enemy Appears

It may seem strange that in this chapter no mention has been made of further trouble from Egypt. One reason is that when Ramses II died, his son Merneptah was so old that it was all he could do in his short reign to take care of his own territory with no foreign entanglements. This weakened Egyptian power rallied somewhat under Ramses III, when a new problem arose—a wave of invading "sea people." These were the Philistines, who seemed to come from nowhere, but probably came from the south Aegean area in what we now call the Greek Islands. The only mention of their source to be found in the Bible is in Amos 9:7:

"Are you not like the Ethiopians to me,
　O people of Israel?" says the Lord.
"Did I not bring up Israel from the land of Egypt,
　and the Philistines from Caphtor and the Syrians from Kir?"

Wherever Caphtor may have been (it was probably Crete), the Egyptians did not want the Philistines. Repulsed by Ramses III, they were shunted to the southwest coastal section of a land which, by one of the ironies of history, was for centuries to bear their name as Palestine. There they entrenched themselves firmly, and made trouble both for Canaanites and Israelites.

The Philistines were a fairly advanced people who were especially skilled in the making of iron implements— chariot wheels, swords, spear tips, and other accessories of warfare. They also developed an effective political organization based on their league of five important cities, each with its own king but with an amphictyonic confederacy. A third advantage which their location gave them was control of the traffic along the coast from the southwest to the north and east. In all these respects, the people of Israel were at a disadvantage.

In the early days of the conquest of Canaan, the Philistines who came in from the opposite direction at about the same time as the people of Israel seem not to have made much trouble. Mention of them is found early in the book of Judges, where we are told that the Israelite Shamgar killed six hundred Philistines with an oxgoad, and thus cleared the roads of marauders that interfered with travel (Judg. 3:31; 5:6). Later we are told, "The

73

people of Israel again did what was evil in the sight of the Lord; and the Lord gave them into the hand of the Philistines for forty years" (Judg. 13:1). Since no account is given of a conflict leading up to such a long bondage, this probably refers to a persistent unsettled state in southwest Canaan due to the Philistine presence. In any case it serves as an introduction to the Samson stories which follow.

While Samson is said to have judged Israel for twenty years (Judg. 16:31), he was never a judge in the typical sense. He was more interested in women than in rulership or military exploits, and the Samson stories as a whole, if not completely folklore, are the least authentic part of the record of the conquest of Canaan. Yet reflections of a blend of religious loyalty with nationalism come through in the story of how the eyeless Samson by his great strength pulled the temple of Dagon down upon both himself and the Philistines seeking to make sport of him (Judg. 16:23-31).

It is not until we come to the book of I Samuel that the contests between Israel and the Philistines reach an acute stage. Toward the end of the eleventh century B.C., as the Philistines took possession of all the routes leading into the hill country, action to resist them became inevitable. The ark of the covenant was kept at Shiloh, which had long been the central sanctuary of the Israelite confederacy. When the contest with the Philistines was going strongly against the Israelites, it was decided to bring the ark to the place of battle with the hope that this would cause the tide to turn. The men of Israel received it with a mighty shout. The Philistines heard this; became alarmed that the gods might be fighting against them; and fought all the harder. Thus the ark not only failed to bring victory

74

but was itself seized by the Philistines. However, so many disasters followed upon its possession that after seven months they were glad to return it (I Sam. 5, 6).[4]

After this decisive victory the Philistines were in possession of a large and important section of central Palestine. Philistine garrisons were stationed at important points. Palestine was fast becoming a Philistine empire. There seemed to be only one answer. Under Samuel's leadership the people decided they must have a king, and this marks the next great watershed in Israel's history.

Notes

1. I have borrowed this term, "the tribal confederacy," from Anderson, *Understanding the Old Testament*, pp. 84-91. It seems an appropriate designation for the bond, more religious than political, that with varying degrees of firmness united the people of Israel during the period of the judges.

   However, it should be recognized that the usual under-standing of the twelve tribes of Israel as each being descended from one of the twelve sons of Jacob is an oversimplification. There were never exactly twelve tribes at any one time. Nor were they all blood descendants of Jacob in the same manner. Joseph's sons, Ephraim and Manasseh, had an Egyptian mother, Asenath (Gen. 41:50-52). Moses was related to the Midianites through his wife, Zipporah, and a band of Kenites, a branch of the Midianites, entered Canaan with the people of Judah in the southern invasion through Jericho (Judg. 1:16). It was Jael, the wife of Heber the Kenite, who killed Sisera to aid Israel (Judg. 5:24). Later the Midianites were to be among Israel's fiercest enemies.

2. The narrator's interest in detail, which so often adds "human interest" touches to otherwise major historic events, appears in the fact that Ehud was a left-handed man who could surprise Eglon by drawing the sword with his left hand from his right thigh.

3. Chemosh was the god of Moab, which lay south of Gilead and at one time had been ruled by Sihon, king of the Amorites, who was defeated by the Israelites before they entered Canaan (Num. 21:21-31). This mention of Chemosh indicates (1) that the Israelites were not yet monotheists but recognized the existence of gods other than their own (i.e., were henotheists), and (2) their basic Deuteronomic conviction that victory in battle was proof of divine favor, defeat an evidence of their sin in going after foreign gods.
4. The sanctuary at Shiloh was apparently destroyed by the Philistines, for the ark was taken on its return to Kiriath-jearim (I Sam. 7:1), where it remained for twenty years until David had it taken to Jerusalem (II Sam. 6:2).

6

And Now a Kingdom

We come now to the United Kingdom—the most glamorous period in Israel's history, despite the fact that it began in a continuation of conflict and ended in disruption into two kingdoms. Its middle period, the reign of King David, was always thereafter to be cited as Israel's most glorious day.

1. Of Samuel and Saul

It is not easy to sort out Samuel's anointing of Saul as king and the ensuing events. Two stories seem to be interwoven which do not agree at all points; yet the main outlines can be traced.

Who was Samuel? He was a remarkable man, and stands in the succession of Moses and Joshua as a great leader who helped to fashion Israel's destiny. Yet he was unlike either. He was the last of the judges and the first of a new line of priestly prophets who exercised great religious as well as political power. He was the last major voice in the tribal confederacy, and the inaugurator of the new era of kingship, though he was never himself a king.

The story of his being dedicated to the Lord by his mother Hannah before his birth, his tutelage at the sanctuary of Shiloh under Eli the chief priest, and his early calling by the Lord to become a prophet, is charmingly told in the first three chapters of I Samuel. His career as a religious and political leader began after the Philistine attack when the ark of the covenant was seized, then returned, and lodged at Kiriath-jearim. After some twenty years of which the history is not related, Samuel, now in his full maturity, called on the people once again to put away their foreign gods and to come together at Mizpah for appropriate rites of repentance and renewal.

The Philistines got word of this assembly, joined battle, and were decisively routed because "the Lord thundered with a mighty voice that day against the Philistines and threw them into confusion" (I Sam. 7:10). Then followed a period in which Israel recovered the cities formerly taken by the Philistines, and there was peace also with the Amorites (I Sam. 7:13-17). Samuel seems to have been given the credit "under the hand of the Lord," and was held in high honor and respect.

As Samuel was getting old he appointed his sons as judges over Israel, but they were not of their father's caliber. They "turned aside after gain; they took bribes and perverted justice" (I Sam. 8:3). This tendency seems then, as now, to have had serious political consequences. Thereupon all the elders of Israel came to Samuel and asked him to appoint a king to govern them like other nations.

Here the accounts diverge. According to one, this displeased Samuel very much, for it seemed that the people were rejecting him. However, another issue was at stake besides Samuel's personal prestige. Israel had always regarded their God, and him alone, as king over them. Was this now to be set aside? Samuel prayed to the

Lord about it, and the answer came, "Hearken to the voice of the people in all that they say to you; for they have not rejected you, but they have rejected me from being king over them" (I Sam. 8:7). Yahweh directed Samuel to let the people have their way but to warn them that with a king they would lose much of their freedom and would have to pay heavy tribute in taxes and services. Thereupon Samuel encountered the tall and handsome Saul who was out seeking his father's asses, invited him to his home at Ramah, and anointed him as prince over Israel.

According to the other account, Saul demonstrated his capacity for leadership when the people of Jabesh-gilead east of the Jordan were again attacked by their old Semitic kinsmen and enemies, the Ammonites. In I Samuel 11 we are told how Saul mustered a great army by the symbol of cutting up a yoke of oxen and sending the pieces throughout all Israel with the warning "Whoever does not come out after Saul and Samuel, so shall it be done to his oxen!" (11:7). The Ammonites were decisively defeated. "So all the people went to Gilgal, and there they made Saul king before the Lord" (11:15).

One reads the story of Saul with mixed feelings. In some respects he proved to be an able and effective king. He drew the tribes together into a closer unity. He reduced the power of the Canaanite strongholds until only Gezer and Jerusalem remained uncaptured. He held in check, though he did not conquer, the Philistines. Yet for all his prowess in battle he was an emotionally disturbed person whose troubles became worse as time went on. Trouble broke out with the aging Samuel, who felt that Saul was assuming too much religious as well as political author-ity. The issue came to a head when in a battle with the

Amalekites Saul insisted he was obeying the voice of the Lord in sparing the life of their king, while Samuel "hewed Agag in pieces before the Lord in Gilgal" (I Sam. 15:17-33).

In retrospect it would appear that Saul was more in the right than Samuel! But the incident caused a fatal break between them, which led Samuel to feel that the Lord no longer wanted Saul to be king, and he anointed David, the son of Jesse of Bethlehem, to replace him (I Sam. 16:1-13)—thus changing the course of history. Naturally Saul became very jealous of David.

Saul's years thereafter were tragic ones. David had lived at the court as a youth, playing his lyre to placate Saul when "an evil spirit" came upon him, and becoming a close friend of Saul's son Jonathan. Now David was Saul's enemy, so persecuted by him that for a time he became an outlaw in the Negeb and later took refuge with the Philistines at Gath. Saul became, if not insane, at least highly irrational. Depressed by the feeling that even Yahweh had deserted him, he still wanted to talk with Samuel, who meanwhile had died. He consulted the witch of Endor—in modern diction a spiritualist medium—and asked her to bring Samuel before him. If he had hoped for counsel or comfort he got none—only that the Lord had given his kingdom to David, that Israel would be given into the hands of the Philistines, and that the next day Saul and his sons would be dead (I Sam. 28:3-19).

This soon happened. In the fateful battle against the Philistines at Mount Gilboa, Saul fought on until the battle was lost; then, his three sons killed and himself badly wounded, he took his own life. The Philistines in derision strung up their bodies on the wall of Beth-shan.

Two gleams of light illumine this sad ending. The men of Jabesh-gilead whom Saul had delivered from the Ammonites risked their lives to give the four bodies honorable burial. And David, now king, mourned the death of Saul and Jonathan in memorable words which are both great poetry and magnanimous in judgment:

> Thy glory, O Israel, is slain upon thy high places!
>   How are the mighty fallen! . . .
>
> Saul and Jonathan, beloved and lovely!
>   In life and in death they were not divided;
> they were swifter than eagles,
>   they were stronger than lions. . . .
>
> How are the mighty fallen,
>   and the weapons of war perished! (II Sam. 1:19-27)

2. David

David did not immediately become king of all Israel. There was a considerable division of loyalty between Judah in the south, where David came from, and the tribes of the north including Gilead east of the Jordan. Upon Saul's death the people of Judah at once accepted David as their king, and he established his capital at Hebron. But the people of the north and east, led by Abner, the commander of Saul's army, insisted that Saul's surviving son, Ishbosheth, was the rightful successor and made him their king with his capital in Gilead. The two kingdoms fought each other for seven years. But upon Abner's defection to David and subsequent murder and Ishbosheth's death the representatives of these northern tribes, probably fearing the Philistines more than David, made a deal with him whereby he became their king.

David was a very able military commander. As soon as he became king of all Israel, the Philistines, who had not bothered him much in his little Hebron kingdom, attacked with great vigor. They were decisively defeated and pushed back into their own territory along the Mediterranean coast (II Sam. 5:17-25). Thus David not only got rid of a long-standing menace but greatly enhanced his prestige. Never again in ancient times did the Philistines give the Hebrews any serious trouble. (Nobody then dreamed that three thousand years later, under the name of Gaza Strip, the area would be seething again.)

This was not David's only conquest. In II Samuel 8 and 10 we are told, in fewer words than we wish we had, of a vast extension of David's kingdom into what was virtually an empire, extending from the Lebanon Mountains almost to the borders of Egypt. Philistia, Moab, Ammon, Edom, Amalek, and Aram (Syria) were captured, apparently in quick succession. All of these peoples except the Philistines were Semites, and hence Israel's hostile relatives as well as neighbors.

Of special importance in view of recent history is David's conquest of Syria with its ancient capital at Damascus. Most of II Samuel 10 is given to an account of this conquest, but the heart of the story is found in a few words in II Samuel 8:3-6. David first conquered the area of Zobah, north of Damascus, seizing thousands of horsemen and foot soldiers. "And when the Syrians of Damascus came to help Hadadezer king of Zobah, David slew twenty-two thousand men of the Syrians. Then David put garrisons in Aram of Damascus; and the Syrians became servants to David and brought tribute. And the Lord gave victory to David wherever he went" (8:5-6).

This occurred in the early part of the tenth century B.C.,

David having reigned from about 1000 to 970 B.C. A little arithmetic will suggest how long the conflict between Israel and Syria has been going on! Syria was again lost to Israel during the reign of Solomon.

David's most lasting achievement has yet to be mentioned. When the Israelites entered Canaan, a line of Canaanite fortresses separated south from central Canaan. In the intervening years, these had all been seized except Jerusalem, then known as Jebus, and Gezer to the west of it on the Philistine border. David captured Jerusalem from the Jebusites and made it his capital. Here his royal palace was built with the help of Hiram king of Tyre, who sent cedars of Lebanon, carpenters, and masons, thus cementing a friendship without the need of battle, which was to appear again in the next generation when Solomon built the temple. Furthermore, David made Jerusalem the religious center of all Israel. He caused the ark of the covenant to be brought there and placed in a tabernacle probably reminiscent of the tent of meeting which housed it in the wilderness journeys. David contemplated building a temple in Jerusalem to serve as the permanent abiding-place of the ark, but was told by Yahweh through the prophet Nathan that this should be done instead by his son and successor.

As for Gezer, David seems to have made no attempt to capture it. It was of some importance in guarding one of the passes between the maritime plain and Jerusalem, but David seems to have been content to let it remain in other hands. Later we are told that one of the pharaohs of Egypt had gone up and captured and burned it, whereupon he gave it as a dowry to Solomon when the latter married his daughter, and Solomon rebuilt it (I Kings 9:16-17).

David was not only a great military commander; he was

a superb diplomat. To have kept his capital at Hebron would have alienated the northern tribes. He could not have moved it to Gilead or anywhere in the north or east without losing the loyalty of Judah. Jerusalem was on the border; it had not been the possession of anybody in Israel until he took it.[1] Now it was "the city of David," and was to remain so for centuries to come.

As everybody knows, Jerusalem is now "the Holy City," sacred to three faiths. In David's time it was not a large city, covering only a few acres on the hill of Ophel in what is now its eastern section. Solomon's temple on Mount Moriah became a sacred spot to the Jew, and on its site is the Dome of the Rock, second only to Mecca as a Muslim shrine. Within it the tourist will be shown an enormous rock on which Abraham is said to have offered Isaac in sacrifice until God stayed his hand, and from which Mohammed took flight to heaven. This rock was once the threshing floor of Araunah, purchased by David from him as an altar to the Lord in gratitude for the staying of a plague that was oppressing Israel (II Sam. 24:15-25).

So Israel was no longer a tribal confederacy with its tribes loosely bound together by a common obligation to their God: it was a nation. Yahweh was still accepted as Israel's leader and guide, but in a different way. There was now an earthly king with great authority over taxes, military conscription, and forced labor. There was one central authority with one capital city which was the seat of both temporal and religious power. For the first time in its history, Israel was not only a self-sufficient nation able to build up trade with other nations, but through conquest of neighboring peoples it had numerous colonies to govern. It looked as if King David "had it made." But did he?

84

Trouble arose through a common human failing—a weakness for women. Though polygamy was a common practice in those days, David went further than most.[2] He acquired six wives while reigning in Hebron, and several others later (II Sam. 3:2-5; 5:13-16). Mention is made also of ten concubines (II Sam. 15:16). This meant a large harem for the people to support. It meant also constant quarreling among the children of the various wives and, as David approached old age, sharp conflict as to the successor.

The most dramatic story recorded is that of David's lust for Bathsheba, the wife of Uriah the Hittite, her pregnancy for which he tried without success to induce Uriah to accept paternity, his strategy to cause Uriah's death, and the stern rebuke he received as Nathan the prophet told the story of the poor man's one ewe lamb (II Sam. 11–12). The sequel is that while this child died, Bathsheba's son Solomon succeeded his father on the throne against the claims of Adonijah, David's surviving firstborn. Another son, Absalom, had led a revolution against his father in which he lost his life, to David's great distress. The first two chapters of I Kings show David as a pathetic figure who in the contest between two groups of supporters yielded to Bathsheba's insistence, in which she had the support of Nathan, that her son be given the throne.

So David, Israel's greatest king, "slept with his fathers," and Solomon reigned in his stead. For the most part, David's weaknesses were forgotten, and it was the qualities that made him great which were later to lead his people to look and long for the coming of a Messiah who would restore Israel to its Davidic greatness. This would be the coming of the kingdom of God.

3. Solomon

Solomon is often referred to as a man of peace and of great wisdom. These terms, if applied to him, must be used in a special sense. There was not much active warfare in his reign, but there was great unrest—what in modern terminology is called "structural violence." He was a brilliant administrator with great commercial and diplomatic skill, but this was exercised in a manner which undermined his kingdom. He was a religious man, yet decidedly secularist when the religion of Yahweh conflicted with commercial or political advantage. In short, all too many of the characteristics of our own time are visible in him.

Solomon's first act upon ascending the throne was to get rid of his rivals—not by his own hand but by executive orders on grounds that scarcely seem capital offenses. Those disposed of included, among others, his elder brother Adonijah, and Joab, David's able and loyal commander-in-chief. The second chapter of I Kings makes pretty gory reading. Then the third gives us Solomon's famous and seemingly humble prayer for wisdom and understanding:

And now, O Lord my God, thou hast made thy servant king in place of David my father, although I am but a little child; I do not know how to go out or come in. And thy servant is in the midst of thy people whom thou hast chosen, a great people, that cannot be numbered or counted for multitude. Give thy servant therefore an understanding mind to govern thy people, that I may discern between good and evil; for who is able to govern this thy great people? (I Kings 3:7-9)

Humbug? Or a genuinely seeking soul? One may draw his own conclusion. Mine is that Solomon meant it as he faced the duties of his office, but lacked the religious stamina to live by this spirit when the crises came. Had this spirit prevailed, his destiny and that of Israel could have been quite different.

We have noted that Solomon inherited from his father what was for those times a very large empire. It included Syria in the north and extended to the Euphrates in the northeast, to the Gulf of Aqaba in the southeast, and to Philistia and almost to Egypt in the southwest. Nothing was then known that would make the Arabian Desert much of a prize, but barring this, most of the territory that has since been fought over was in David's possession. With Solomon's coming to power, the empire began almost immediately to shrink. The first to break away was Edom, the Esau country south of Moab, but, fortunately for Solomon's later commercial enterprises, he was able to retain access to the Gulf of Aqaba, Israel's only natural seaport (I Kings 11:14-22).

The next to be lost was David's hard-won kingdom of Syria with Damascus its strategic center (I Kings 11:23-25). King Rezon I of Damascus established a dynasty which lasted for two centuries, and which opened the way to numerous subsequent clashes between Syrians and Hebrews. We shall meet these again and again in Israel's later history.

There is no evidence that Solomon made much resistance to the capture of these two important centers. He may have thought it not worthwhile to resist. But whatever it did to his prestige, he lost revenue, which meant higher taxes for his own people. He had already made slaves of the former Canaanites who had not become amalgamated with the Hebrews—"all the people who were left of the Amorites, the Hittites, the Perizzites, the

Hivites, and the Jebusites, who were not of the people of Israel" (I Kings 9:20)—and it was mainly they who served as forced labor for his great building enterprises.

We come now to the achievements on which Solomon's fame chiefly rests. At the head of these is his building of the temple. Though it was destroyed by Nebuchadnezzar's armies about 375 years after its completion, its site is still revered. Compared with modern cathedrals it was not a very large structure (about ninety by thirty by forty-five feet).[3] Built by Phoenician architects, it bore some Canaanite art work; still, it was the house of Israel's God. The ark was placed in it with a ceremonial procession and the temple was duly dedicated with a moving prayer by Solomon (I Kings 8). Through the centuries the achievement of building the temple has lent a glow to Solomon's memory.

Other buildings were erected around the temple: the king's palace, another for the wife who was Pharaoh's daughter, and some government buildings. These helped to beautify the city. More famous, however, were the fortifications of several "chariot cities" throughout Solomon's domain. By this time the people of Israel had adopted the Canaanite and Philistine use of horse-drawn chariots, not only for military security but to protect the trade routes which crisscrossed the country. Extensive excavations at Megiddo, at the western end of the Plain of Esdraelon, have unearthed massive walls, ramparts, and stables that could have housed 150 chariots and 450 to 500 horses.

This leads to a second of Solomon's major achievements—in the realm of commerce. He was a great "horse trader," importing horses and chariots from Egypt and Cilicia and selling them, doubtless at a good profit, to the kings of the Hittites and of Syria (I Kings 10:28-29). More important, however, was the opening of a seaport at Ezion-geber on the Gulf of Aqaba. Thanks to his friendship with Hiram of Tyre, Solomon's ships sailed with the Phoenicians to distant ports, sometimes requiring three years to make the circuit (I Kings 10:22). This brought to Israel such luxuries as "gold, silver, ivory, apes, and peacocks." But imports require exports, and Solomon shrewdly capitalized on the mineral resources of his territory: Copper and iron ore were taken from the Arabah section near the gulf and from Sinai, and Solomon established a smelting plant at Ezion-geber. This has been excavated by Nelson Glueck, who has called it "the Pittsburgh of Palestine" and conjectures that the purpose of the Queen of Sheba's visit was to negotiate a commercial treaty.[4]

The third main area of Solomon's kingship was his international diplomacy. This took two principal forms. One was to curry favor or at least induce awe among the neighboring rulers. We are told that "King Solomon excelled all the kings of the earth in riches and in wisdom," and that many besides the Queen of Sheba came to him bringing lavish gifts (I Kings 10:23-25). This accounts in considerable measure for the fact that, except for his early losses of territory, Solomon's reign was remarkably free from overt wars.

But this was not his only strategy. A major part of Solomon's policy was to make diplomatic marriages. His marriage to Pharaoh's daughter gave him not only the city of Gezer as a dowry, but also peace with Egypt. This happened repeatedly. We are told that "King Solomon loved many foreign women: the daughter of Pharaoh, and Moabite, Ammonite, Edomite, Sidonian, and Hittite women" (I Kings 11:1). The people of Israel had been forbidden to marry into these nations, yet Solomon did so freely, and while "seven hundred wives, princesses, and three hundred concubines" (11:3) may be an exaggeration, he seems to have maintained an enormous household—at his subjects' expense. Furthermore, in addition to the temple to Yahweh he erected pagan shrines for his wives' various religious and cultural backgrounds.

All this was costing the people a vast amount in taxes and forced labor. Revolt was brewing. At Solomon's death it came to a head. Then there were two kingdoms instead of one.

Notes

1. This action may be favorably compared with the wisdom of our Founding Fathers in establishing the capital of the United States, not in Philadelphia where the first important political steps were taken, but in a new city not located in any of the states.
2. Adultery was strictly condemned, not only in the Ten Commandments, but in each of the three major law codes: the Covenant Code (Exod. 20:14; cf. 22:16); the Deuteronomic Code (Deut. 5:18; cf. Deut. 22:22), where it becomes a capital offense; and the Holiness Code (Lev. 18:14-20). However, no prohibition of polygamy is found in the Old Testament. In Deuteronomy 21:15-17 its existence is assumed, and a prohibition is given against discriminating in inheritance against the first wife's offspring even if she is disliked.
3. The dimensions of the temple are given (I Kings 6:2) as "sixty cubits long, twenty cubits wide, and thirty cubits high." A cubit, usually estimated as eighteen inches, was the distance from the elbow to the tip of the middle finger. In I Kings 6–8 is a detailed description of the temple and its furnishings.
4. See Nelson Glueck, *The Other Side of the Jordan* (New Haven: American Schools of Oriental Research, 1940), pp. 50-113.

7

Then There Were Two Kingdoms

David's establishment of the United Kingdom, with Jerusalem as its capital, was an achievement unique in the history of the Holy Land. This was so because for the first time the land was both united and ruled by its own inhabitants. Previously this area had either been divided into separate tribal regions or city-states, or it had been ruled by a foreign power. But David's achievement was short-lived. It lasted less than a century, and to this day there has been only one more period when the Holy Land has enjoyed unity under its own power as in the days of David and Solomon. This was in the era of the Maccabees in the second and first centuries B.C.

The partition of the land which has been in effect since 1948 is between east and west. The state of Israel is a long north-south strip of land on the west, with the Arab state of the Hashemite Kingdom of Jordan lying parallel on the east. The boundary between the two is a crazy, jagged line running from Lebanon in the north to the Sinai Peninsula in the south. The partition following Solomon's reign was to be between north and south. The northern kingdom was called Israel, and the southern kingdom was known as Judah. The east-west boundary between the two was a fluctuating line drawn a few miles north of Jerusalem and running from the Mediterranean Sea on the west across the Jordan River and into Transjordan as far as the desert on the east. The clashes of Israel and Judah with each other and with the surrounding nations illustrate the process which in our time has caused four wars in this area within one century.

Upon the death of Solomon his son Rehoboam was immediately ready to assume the kingship. Apparently a dynastic father-to-son succession was accepted without question in Judah, the southern section of the kingdom, perhaps in part because this area had received favored status in Solomon's economic policies. But now the king-to-be must go to the ancient tribal center of the north, Shechem, to secure the continued allegiance of the northerners. Hence, as the book of I Kings puts it, "Rehoboam went to Shechem, for all Israel had come to Shechem to make him king" (12:1). However, if such were the people's intent in coming to this representative assembly, the whole plan went awry.

Rehoboam may have been stupidly unaware of the depth of resentment in the north toward a dynastic rule from the south and especially against the oppressive forced labor policies which were in effect. In any case, the young monarch's arrogant answer the third day, "My father chastised you with whips, but I will chastise you with scorpions" (12:14), brought a renewal of the cry which his grandfather David had heard:

> What portion have we in David?
> We have no inheritance in the son of Jesse.
> To your tents, O Israel!
> Look now to your own house, David. (12:16)

So determined was the northerners' revolt that they stoned to death the "taskmaster over the forced labor" whom Rehoboam sent to subdue them, and Rehoboam himself literally fled in his chariot back to Jerusalem (12:18). "So Israel has been in rebellion against the house of David to this day," comments the biblical author, writing perhaps four centuries later (12:19). And Rehoboam was subsequently dissuaded by the prophet Shemaiah from using his force of "a hundred and eighty thousand chosen warriors" to attempt to compel the northerners' allegiance (12:21-24).

Thus the united nation founded by David broke apart into two rival minor kingdoms. For the next two hundred years, until the northern kingdom, Israel, fell to outside forces, these two states were at times in tenuous alliance with each other, at times bitter rivals on the battlefield, and frequently embroiled in conflicts with outside states—a situation in some ways comparable to the present-day situation in the Holy Land. For clarity of perspective on the main outlines of the story, we shall first follow the fortunes of the larger and economically and politically more important of the two, Israel, until its demise in 722 B.C.

1. Israel

Whereas King David and his descendants managed to continue one line of rule in Jerusalem for four centuries, the rulers of the northern kingdom constituted a series of dynasties interrupted by coups d'etat and not infrequent political chaos. The first of these dynasties was established by the human engineer of the original rebellion, Jeroboam son of Nebat. This onetime labor leader had earlier been King Solomon's appointee as overseer of the forced labor of the northerners, "the house of Joseph" (I

93

Kings 11:28). But when Solomon had learned that this able young man had political ambitions of his own—perhaps to become king of the north at the instigation of the prophet Ahijah of Shiloh—Jeroboam had had to flee for his life to Egypt. There he had married the pharaoh Shishak's sister-in-law, possibly following the precedent set by his patriarchal ancestor Joseph.

Doubtless it was Jeroboam's organizing genius that readily took advantage of Rehoboam's insensitivity toward the northerners at the Shechem assembly. Thus he wrested from the Davidic line of rule the "ten tribes of the north," as the northern kingdom popularly known as Israel was subsequently commonly termed. This act left to David's line only one quite significant tribe, Judah, with one small satellite tribe, Simeon.

When Jeroboam began his twenty-one-year reign over Israel, his first task was to create a new national state which could permit no residual allegiance to Jerusalem, the site of David's throne and Solomon's temple. Astutely he chose as his capital city ancient Shechem, the onetime Canaanite royal center, located at the important crossroads of the north and remembered as the traditional site of Abraham's first stop in Canaan (Gen. 12:6).[1]

Jeroboam further chose the ancient shrines of Dan and Bethel as religious capitals, to which his subjects were to come for worship instead of going south to the Davidic line's royal shrine at Jerusalem. This selection was perhaps his most outstanding act of good judgment. These centers were respectively at the northern and southern extremities of his new kingdom. But, more important, each had superb claims to religious loyalty. Dan's priesthood presumably dated back to Moses (Judg. 18:30). At Bethel Jacob, whose other name was Israel, had had a vision of God and his angels on the "ladder"—really a ramp leading up to heaven (Gen. 28). The "two calves of gold" which Jeroboam placed at these two royal shrines (I Kings 12:28-29) were probably understood by the king to be simply the two gorgeous bull-image platforms upon which stood the invisible national God, Yahweh. But these two images at the northern shrines rivaling Jerusalem came to be regarded as idols, as symbols of the Canaanite fertility god Baal, and hence as the source of evil apostasy from the true worship of Yahweh. Thus before his death King Jeroboam, not unlike Saul earlier, was repudiated by the prophets who had encouraged his original revolution.

Jeroboam was successful in establishing a kingdom in the north whose leadership was chosen by divine designation through the prophets and by popular consent. But when, upon Jeroboam's death, his son Nadab tried to succeed him, he was soon assassinated by one Baasha, presumably an officer in his army. Baasha in his turn ruled for nearly a quarter of a century from his capital at Tirzah. When Baasha died his son Elah was assassinated by an army officer, Zimri, who, unable to secure the throne and finding himself, after only a week, besieged in Tirzah by Omri, the commander of the army, committed suicide. Thus the first fifty years of Israel's existence as a nation ended in a period of civil war.

Omri at last managed to stabilize the rule of the kingdom and to establish a dynastic family—Omri, Ahab, Ahaziah, Jehoram—which ruled for almost another half-century. It was during this period that the northern kingdom first became heavily embroiled in the military conflicts within the larger world outside the Palestinian corridor. During the earlier reigns of Jeroboam and Baasha there had been some struggles over Israel's relations with neighboring states to the east and north, but the chief struggles had been with Judah over the exact boundary between the northern and southern kingdoms. Omri reigned for twelve years, and although his reign is given relatively little attention in the Bible (I Kings 16:22-28), his brief but able rule brought him international fame, for in the Assyrian records for many subsequent years Israel is referred to as "the land of the house of Omri."

Omri's most notable internal achievement was the establishment of Samaria as his capital. Like David's capital, Jerusalem, the hill of Samaria was a readily defendable fortress. Unlike Jerusalem, however, it was not a previously known city. On this hill overlooking the territory for miles around, the city built by Omri and his successors was to remain significant for centuries, into the New Testament period and beyond.

Israel's relations with her immediate neighbors during the reigns of Omri and his son Ahab demand our attention. These immediate neighbors—Phoenicia to the north, Syria, or Aram, to the northeast, Ammon and Moab to the east and southeast—correspond roughly to their present-day counterparts.[2]

Perhaps most notable was Omri's defeat of the Moabites, as admitted by King Mesha of Moab on his famous record known as the Moabite Stone. Throughout Ahab's reign this neighbor to the southeast remained a vassal state of Israel. It was during the reign of Ahab's son Jehoram that the Moabites won their freedom in a definitive war in which the Moabite king offered his son as a human sacrifice (II Kings 3:4-27).

War between Israel and Syria, between Samaria and Damascus—with Judah and its capital, Jerusalem, sometimes Samaria's ally, sometimes its enemy—seemed almost the order of the day through these decades in the ninth and the early eighth centuries B.C. During the fifty years of Israel's instability previous to Omri's rule, Damascus had become the dominant power of Palestine and Syria under the forty-year rule of the Syrian king Ben-hadad. Although this monarch had earlier harassed King Baasha of Israel, and in about the twelfth year of Ahab's reign he even besieged Samaria, Ahab was able to defeat the Syrians in a battle east of the Sea of Galilee the following year.

With the Phoenicians Omri sealed an alliance by the marriage of his son Ahab to Jezebel, daughter of the king of Sidon (I Kings 16:31). Such an alliance had the advantage of securing Phoenician help against Damascus in a balance-of-power move among these small states. However, such were the changing interrelationships that after his defeat of the Syrians, Ahab not only treated the captive Syrian king Ben-hadad with amazing leniency, but soon became his ally!

And the reason was not far to seek: looming upon the eastern horizon was the threatening power of Assyria.[3] This nation's various thrusts westward during the subsequent two centuries were to be a continuing menace to the peace of Palestine; hence during the reign of Ahab the little states of the area formed a coalition to stop the eastern juggernaut. And, mirabile dictu, after the Assyrian king Shalmaneser III had pushed southward through Syria, despite Assyrian claims of victory the little coalition was able to stop him in a pitched battle at Qarqar on the Orontes River. This crucial victory was in no small part due to Ahab's contribution of two thousand chariots and ten thousand foot soldiers (according to Shal-

97

maneser's own records, for these are not mentioned in the Bible). Yet scarcely had the Assyrian menace withdrawn than the coalition fell apart. When Ben-hadad refused to carry out certain trade agreements, Israel and Syria were again at each other's throat, and Ahab met his death in a battle at the border city of Ramoth-gilead, as predicted by the prophet Micaiah son of Imlah (I Kings 22).

Of all her relations with her neighbors, Israel's alliance with Phoenicia was the most crucial for her life. Her struggle with Phoenicia was not military. It was religious. The conflict was between Israel's national covenant loyalty to Yahweh and the worship of the god Baal, especially as the latter was the Tyrian deity of Queen Jezebel and her followers. The great protagonist for Yahweh was the prophet Elijah. His contest with the Baal worshipers on Mount Carmel (I Kings 18) and his championship of the rights of the peasant Naboth against despotic monarchic power (I Kings 21) were most notable. In this cultural conflict between the prophets of Baal and the prophets of Yahweh, no matter how critical the Yahweh prophet may have been of the royal house of Israel and its sins, he never forsook his own people in favor of the people of Damascus or Tyre.

The bloodiest revolution of all took place at the instigation of Elisha, successor to the prophet Elijah. This swept away the dynasty of Omri and put another army general, Jehu, on the throne of Israel. And the dynasty of Jehu was to remain on the throne for a century, actually half of the total existence of Israel as a separate kingdom.

In this bloody purge Queen Jezebel was thrown to the scavenger dogs, seventy sons of Ahab were massacred, and the host of Baal prophets and priests were murdered—all in the name of Yahweh. Although these drastic measures, later to be repudiated by the prophet Hosea, probably saved Israel from going further down the road of religious syncretism with the pagan culture of Baalism, their cost was heavy in human relationships. The reaction of many within the kingdom itself must surely have been bitter. Needless to say, by the insult to the royal deity of Phoenicia friendly relations with that country were broken. And friendly relations with the southern kingdom of Judah were ruined by Jehu's murder of Judah's king Ahaziah (II Kings 9:1-28).

As a result of these failures in human relations, for the next fifty years Jehu's nation was largely paralyzed internally and unable to cope with external international forces. The immediate effect of Israel's weakness was Jehu's capitulation to the renewed westward invasion of the Assyrians. In fact, the Israelite king chose alliance with the farther enemy, Assyria, for security against the nearer one, Syria. One of the best-known monuments from biblical times is Shalmaneser's Black Obelisk, which depicts King Jehu with his tribute bearers behind him bowing down in the dust before the Assyrian monarch. As Jehu is named on this monument, he is the only named person of biblical times to appear on any contemporary artifact yet found by archaeologists.

Soon afterward, the Assyrians temporarily gave up their westward expansion, and Israel fell into the hands of a now strong Damascus and lost all her Transjordan territory to Syria. The result was that Jehu's son Jehoahaz was permitted only a bodyguard of "fifty horsemen and ten chariots" plus a police force of "ten thousand footmen" (II Kings 13:7). The series of wars between Israel and her Syrian neighbor in these years were the basis for such vivid biblical accounts as the story of Naaman and

99

the prophet Elisha (II Kings 5) and the narrative of the terrible famine in besieged Samaria when starving families ate boiled infants (II Kings 6:24-31).

Such were the struggles of Israel with the surrounding nations. There were other conflicts both with Assyria and Syria and with the southern kingdom of Judah which need not detain us. But at last the forty-one-year reign of Jehu's great-grandson Jeroboam (ca. 786–746 B.C.),[4] commonly called Jeroboam II to distinguish him from the founder of the northern kingdom, brought peace and unprecedented prosperity. Partly because both Assyria and Syria were involved in internal affairs, Jeroboam II was able to enlarge Israel's borders again to the northern and eastern boundaries of Solomon's empire (II Kings 14:25). In so doing the king was supported by the nationalistic prophet Jonah, whose story in the postexilic book of Jonah raises questions as to this reluctant prophet's understanding of God.

By all odds the most famous prophet of Jeroboam's day was Amos, the southern herdsman who was expelled from the national sanctuary at Bethel for his subversive activities (Amos 7:10-17). It was this pioneer prophet of God's demands for justice and righteousness who, with his northern contemporary Hosea, saw through the veneer of ivory-palace prosperity for the wealthy in both marketplace and sanctuary to the base exploitation of the humble poor. Not simply for humanitarian reasons, but because Israel's conduct violated God's people's covenant of loyalty to their God who had brought their ancestors out of the bondage of Egypt, Amos predicted that "the day of the Lord" would be the day of Yahweh's coming in awful judgment.

Following Jeroboam's reign, Israel's doom was rather

rapidly sealed. As the prophet Hosea testified, the final twenty-five years until Samaria's fall in 722 B.C. were a period of turbulent political and social upheaval when king after king gained the throne by assassinating his predecessor. During this time an Assyrian monarch, Tiglath-pileser III, known as Pul to the Babylonians, whose king he became, and in the biblical narrative (II Kings 15:19), adopted a new strategy in his conquests. When he seized territory, he exiled many local inhabitants to far-flung parts of his empire and resettled the area with other captive peoples (15:29).[5]

In the political anarchy of these days all the frantic attempts to save the independence of Israel, with or without her neighbors, failed: Menahem's huge payment of unbearably high tribute to Assyria (II Kings 15:19-20); Pekah's alliance with Rezin king of Syria against Judah in return for Syria's defense against Assyria (II Kings 15:37; 16:5; Isa. 7:1-9); Hoshea's final appeal for Egyptian help (II Kings 17:4). This last, desperate measure was Israel's suicide. Damascus had fallen to Tiglath-pileser in 732 B.C. When Shalmaneser V captured almost all of Israel in 724, the city of Samaria valiantly held out for over two years. Finally Sargon II took the city in 722/721, and, according to Assyrian records, he deported 27,290 of its citizens to the East, replacing them with conquered peoples from other parts of the empire. So, technically, were lost forever "the ten tribes of Israel" (II Kings 17:23-41).[6]

2. Judah

The smaller but religiously highly significant southern kingdom, Judah, with its capital, Jerusalem, was destined to live on for almost another century and a half. It was in

Judah that the great religious traditions, many of which doubtless had originated in the north, were to survive and be passed on to posterity.

During the preceding two hundred years, when Israel and Judah were rival states, the role of Judah was often that of a satellite of its northern counterpart, but on occasion there was bitter enmity between the two. Most important, however, is the fact that in the southern kingdom the rule of the dynasty of David lasted for four hundred years—a span of time phenomenal in world history which understandably gave rise to messianic hopes still alive in our own day.

If, despite the advice of the prophets, Solomon's son Rehoboam had hoped to reconquer the northern kingdom when it revolted against him, his hopes would soon have been dashed by a very costly invasion from Egypt. Pharaoh Shishak's terrific devastation of Palestine (I Kings 14:25-28), even into Israel in the north, as his inscription on the temple of Karnak indicates, was doubtless an attempt to reestablish the Egyptian Empire in hither Asia. But Egypt soon was in decline and did not harass Judah again for 150 years.

During his forty-year reign over Judah Rehoboam's grandson Asa was almost continually at war with Israel. At one time, when Israel's armies penetrated into Judah as far as Ramah, only five miles north of Jerusalem, Asa even foolishly appealed to Syria for help against his northern rival. But Asa's son and successor Jehoshaphat joined with Israel against Syria. He did so in part because the power of Israel under Omri and Ahab could hardly be withstood, especially when Jehoshaphat's own son Jehoram was married to Athaliah, the daughter of Ahab and his infamous wife Jezebel (II Kings 8:18).

This intermarriage between the royal families of Judah and Israel brought an abrupt end to the good relations between the rival kingdoms. For at about the time that Jehu staged his bloody purge in Israel, Queen Athaliah of Judah murdered the claimants to Judah's throne following the death of her son Ahaziah, and ruled alone in Jerusalem for six years—the only break in Jerusalem's Davidic ruling line from approximately 1000 to 586 B.C. But the Jerusalem priests, loyal to Yahweh, abruptly ended this Baal-worshiping northern woman's rule by assassination and restored the Judean throne to the rightful Davidic heir, seven-year-old Joash, who had successfully been kept in hiding until the right moment (II Kings 11).

The climax of Judah's humiliation by powerful Israel came when King Amaziah of Judah, Joash's son, was taken prisoner by his northern rival, King Jehoash of Israel, and the northerners invaded and pillaged Jerusalem itself (II Kings 14:11-14). At last, however, peace between the two kingdoms was restored in the middle of the eighth century B.C., during the forty-year reign of Uzziah of Judah (ca. 783–742 B.C.), a period of rule almost equally paralleling the prosperous reign of Jeroboam II of Israel. This prosperous era for both Israel and Judah could be compared with that of King Solomon as regards the establishment of trade routes and the extension of Judah's territory to the southern port of Ezion-geber (modern Elath) on the Gulf of Aqaba.

Judah's struggle with Israel was resumed when, during the reign of Uzziah's grandson, young King Ahaz, in the Syro-Ephraimite crisis of 735–734, the southern kingdom was challenged to join the coalition of Israel and Syria against the menace of Assyria, and refused. As the prophet Isaiah of Jerusalem counseled against such an

103

alliance, he was scornful of Ahaz's complete submission to Assyria in calling for this great power's help when the kings of Israel and Syria subsequently invaded Judah. By his action Ahaz avoided bringing upon his nation such a calamity as ended the northern kingdom in 722–721. Nevertheless his complete sellout politically, militarily, and especially religiously, to this demanding foe from the east (II Kings 16:10-18), even to offering his own son as a human sacrifice, brought upon him the historical verdict of being incomparably pagan (II Kings 16:2-4).

The fall of its larger northern neighbor Israel, after two centuries of independent existence, sent shock waves into little Judah. Hence in the latter's final 150 years, much of its energy was consumed in frantic concern over the best means of survival. Not altogether unlike the present situation in the Middle East, this little buffer state was caught between two great poles of power: Egypt to the southwest, and the dominant state in the Mesopotamian valley to the northeast, first Assyria and then Babylonia. In the last quarter of the eighth century B.C. the pro-Egyptian party and the pro-Assyrian party in Judean politics struggled with each other for supremacy, and the statesman-prophet Isaiah declared the futility of dependence upon either foreign power.

King Hezekiah, son and successor of Ahaz, declared Judah's religious independence from Assyria by instituting reform and throwing off the yoke of Ahaz's worship of Assyrian gods. Enticed on the one hand by the expectation of Egyptian help from the west, much against the judgment of Isaiah (Isa. 20:1-6; 30:1-7; 31:1-3), and encouraged on the other hand by the rising power of the new Chaldean dynasty in Babylon, Assyria's neighbor foe in the southern Tigris-Euphrates valley, Hezekiah revolted against Assyria in concert with nearby buffer states. But by the end of the century the Assyrian monarch Sennacherib marched west and effectively quelled the revolt. According to his own record he felled forty-six walled cities of Judah and then besieged Jerusalem. Fearing such an eventuality, Hezekiah had taken the precaution of having the quarter-mile-long Siloam tunnel dug in the solid rock under Jerusalem to assure the city's water supply.

Hezekiah's Judah was ravaged by Sennacherib,[7] and the king was even forced to strip the temple to pay a huge tribute to Assyria (II Kings 18:13-16). Nevertheless, as celebrated in the biblical narrative (II Kings 19:35-36; Isa. 37:36-37) and in one of Lord Byron's most famous poems, and verified by Sennacherib's silence in his record, Jerusalem was seemingly miraculously spared.

Perhaps Sennacherib suddenly lifted the siege of the city because of an outbreak of bubonic plague in his army, as the Greek historian Herodotus seems to suggest. In any case, the fact that Jerusalem was not taken by the mightiest military power of those days gave rise to the popular view that it was inviolable. God would never permit pagan power to overthrow his holy temple and his holy city! Because of this notion Jeremiah nearly met his death a century later, accused of political and religious treason because he dared to dispute the doctrine of Jerusalem's holy inviolability (Jer. 7:1-15; 26:1-15, 24). This prophet's life was spared in part because of the precedent set when King Hezekiah had not condemned the rural prophet Micah to death for announcing Jerusalem's destruction (Mic. 3:9-12; Jer. 26:16-19).

For the next seventy-five years after Hezekiah's capitulation to Assyria—indeed throughout three-quarters of the seventh century B.C.—the kingdom of Judah was but a vassal state of Assyria. Especially during the fifty-five-year reign of Hezekiah's son Manasseh, when the expanding Assyrian Empire even swallowed up Egypt, true worship of Yahweh in Judah had to go underground to escape the tyranny of Assyrian religious and political domination. The biblical writers blamed the subsequent fall of Jerusalem on the awful sins of apostasy of Manasseh's days (II Kings 21:10-15). Even the reforms of the good King Josiah, Manasseh's grandson, with which Deuteronomy is associated as the probable book found in the temple in 621 B.C. (II Kings 22:3–23:27), could not avert the final disaster.

Actually these last decades of Judah's existence were a period of almost continual international turmoil. Assyria had passed its zenith. Its decline was due both to internal strife and to invasions from the north and east by the Medes and the Scythians. The latter were the probable "foe from the north" which called forth the prophets Jeremiah and Zephaniah.

But the greatest menace to Assyria—and soon to the little buffer states along the Mediterranean—was the rapidly rising power of Babylon as the Chaldean Neo-Babylonian Empire was coming into being. When in 612 B.C. the Medes and Babylonians destroyed Nineveh, the Assyrian capital, Judah and other little states, longtime victims of the Assyrians, rejoiced—witness the taunt song of the prophet Nahum over the death of that "bloody city, all full of lies and booty" as but the long-delayed justice of God (Nahum 1:2-3; 3:1). Such rejoicing was to be short-lived, however, for now the new Babylonian-Chaldean power, which had rescued little Judah from the might of Assyria, was to become the new and even more

106

deadly foe.[8] The prophet Habakkuk cried out in amazement as truth stranger than fiction took shape. He could
scarcely believe that God should be "rousing the Chaldeans, / that bitter and hasty nation, / who march through
the breadth of the earth, / to seize habitations not their
own" (Hab. 1:5-6).

Into the fray promptly entered Egypt, ready to capitalize
on a chance to reestablish imperial ambitions in hither
Asia. Pharaoh Neco, hoping to assist falling Assyria,
rushed to the Euphrates to fight against the Chaldeans. On
the way he killed King Josiah of Judah at Megiddo, for the
Judean king was manifestly anti-Assyrian (II Kings 23:29).

Thus Judah, which had regained national independence during the reign of Josiah, and had even apparently
regained much of the territory of the former northern
kingdom of Israel, again became a vassal state. This time
Egypt, not Assyria, was her overlord.

When Josiah was killed, the people's choice to succeed
this beloved king was his son, twenty-three-year-old
Jehoahaz. But after a reign of only three months, the
young king was deported to Egypt by Pharaoh Neco, who
appointed Jehoiakim, Jehoahaz' older brother, King of
Judah in his stead (II Kings 23:30-35). Four years later, in
605 B.C., the Egyptian army was soundly defeated by King
Nebuchadnezzar of Babylon in a pitched battle at
Carchemish, on the great western bend of the Euphrates
River, and the Egyptians met defeat again later near
Hamath in Syria. When the Babylonian army had
penetrated southward to the Philistine plain Jehoiakim
transferred his allegiance from Egypt to Babylon.

Unfortunately King Jehoiakim was never to be trusted,
according to the prophet Jeremiah (Jer. 22:13-19). A few
years later, once again hopeful of Egyptian help, he made

the fatal mistake of revolting against Babylon (II Kings 24:1). Apparently the king died during Nebuchadnezzar's subsequent siege of Jerusalem. And after only three months' reign Jehoiakim's eighteen-year-old son, Jehoiachin, who had succeeded him, surrendered to Nebuchadnezzar on March 16, 597 B.C. This exact date is known to us from the account in the archaeologically very significant contemporary Babylonian Chronicle. According to the biblical account, the young king, high officials, and leading citizens of Jerusalem to the number of ten thousand were carried away captive to Babylon (II Kings 24:8-16).

Nebuchadnezzar's appointment of a third son of Josiah, given the throne name of Zedekiah,[9] as king over Judah (II Kings 24:17) was from his perspective an act of wise benevolence to a subject state. But when later, unable to withstand the hot-headed princes of the palace, and contrary to the advice of Jeremiah, Zedekiah also foolishly revolted, Nebuchadnezzar unleashed his fury on Jerusalem. From January, 588, to July, 586, the city withstood the Babylonian siege. But finally Zedekiah was captured, his sons were killed before his eyes, and he was blinded and carried off to Babylon in chains along with many more citizens of Jerusalem. Then the city—its walls, its palace, its temple—was razed. Only a disillusioned few inhabitants remained. And soon, after an impetuous assassination, many of them fled south to Egypt (II Kings 25:1-26; Jer. 52:1-30).

The impossible had happened. For more than four hundred years Jerusalem had stood through thick and thin, through prosperity and adversity, through good times and bad. But now God's nation, God's temple were no more. The end had come. The curtain of God's wrath had fallen, surely never to rise again.

Notes

1. This ancient city was situated just a short distance east of modern Nablus, center of present-day local Palestinian concern on the West Bank. It was strategically located in the east-west pass between Mounts Gerizim and Ebal and on the main north-south road through the central highlands.
2. Phoenicia, with its southern cities of Tyre and Sidon, corresponds roughly to present-day Lebanon. Syria, with its ancient capital Damascus, is roughly present-day Syria. Ancient Rabbath-Ammon, capital of Ammon, is modern Amman, capital of the Hashemite Kingdom of Jordan.
3. This important north Mesopotamian empire, with its capital at various times Asshur, Dur Sharrukin (or Khorsabad), and Nineveh, occupied the northern portion of what is now Iraq. The site of ancient Nineveh lies just east of present-day Mosul.
4. The chronology of the kings of Israel and Judah presents difficult problems. These dates, as well as others in this book, are those of a chronology developed by W. F. Albright and accepted by such scholars as John Bright, H. B. MacLean, and H. H. Rowley. An alternative chronology developed by E. R. Thiele, in which Jeroboam II's dates are 782–753 B.C., is used in *The Interpreter's One-Volume Commentary on the Bible*, ed. Charles M. Laymon (Nashville: Abingdon Press, 1971).
5. Importation into Israel of captive peoples from other conquered areas eventually resulted in intermingling and intermarriage. Hence, in part, the contempt for the "half-breed" Samaritans by ethnically conscious Jews in later postexilic and New Testament times.
6. This statement is historically and politically accurate. But the later role of the Samaritans and the political unification under the Maccabees must be taken into account in subsequent centuries.

7. Whether in only one campaign in 701 B.C. or also in a second a few years later is a matter of historical debate.
8. Compare the way in which Russia, our ally in World War II which stopped the German juggernaut at Stalingrad in 1945, became the new enemy in the 1950s with the fear of a World War III.
9. The throne names, rather than the personal names, of the Judean kings are given in our account in order to avoid a confusing and unnecessary multiplication of names.

8

Conquered but Undefeated

To any but the most naïve optimists in Jeremiah's and Ezekiel's day, the fall of Jerusalem to Nebuchadnezzar's Babylon had meant the inevitable and irrevocable death of Yahweh's nation Judah. Despite the promises to King David's line, which had occupied Jerusalem's throne for over four centuries—and Solomon's temple had stood for almost as long—the nation had now died. Surely few, if any, Judean exiles torn from their homeland in those fateful days, their dreams dashed to the ground, could ever have hoped that their nation would rise again.

But it is the resurrection of this nation and its continued life for some seven centuries more in the biblical period which is the theme of our discussion in this present chapter. Judah survived with a strong sense of national destiny. Yet its new life was an almost continuous struggle against division within and foes without. Furthermore, except for approximately a century, this little country was continually under the thumb of a succession of conquerors. The outline of these vicissitudes invites some instructive comparisons to the struggles in the Middle East today.

1. The Jews Under the Persians

The death of the nation of Judah in the late sixth century B.C., as we have seen, resulted in the dispersion of many

Jews from their Palestinian homeland to Babylon, to Egypt, and elsewhere in the world. But because they originated in Judah, from this time on Jews, rather than the older Hebrews or Israelites, becomes an appropriate name for all these people, whether they continued to live in Jerusalem and its environs or had moved elsewhere in the world.[1]

A major result, both immediate and long-term, of this period of exile away from Judah was the beginnings and growth of what is termed Diaspora Judaism. This Judaism of the Dispersion consisted of the Jews scattered over the world, who were usually congregated in urban centers in Babylonia, Egypt, or elsewhere. Little is known of the numbers of these eventually non-Palestinian Jews, but in New Testament times it is estimated that there were six times as many Jews living outside Palestine as in that little eastern Mediterranean country itself. Hence the tremendous crowds in New Testament Jerusalem at Passover and Pentecost. On these festival occasions Jews from "every nation under heaven" (Acts 2:5) made their pilgrimage to the Holy City.

Many of the Jewish exiles in Babylon settled there permanently, in only partial accordance with Jeremiah's advice (Jer. 29:1-7). Some of them adopted the Babylonian religion and had no interest in returning to their homeland. Others adapted their ancestral faith to their new environment. Eventually from these beginnings a number of onetime Jewish exiles in Babylon became involved locally in various professions, in banking, and in international trade. For them and others Aramaic became the language of business and international affairs. In fact an earlier Hebrew script is now replaced by the twenty-two so-called square letters of the Aramaic alphabet, which Aramaic script is used in the Dead Sea Scrolls. The importance of the non-Palestinian Jewish centers in the subsequent centuries is seen in the rise and significance of the synagogue as everywhere the local expression of Jewish religious and communal life. The compilation of such tremendous works as the Babylonian Talmud also testifies to the importance of Diaspora Judaism.

Some of the exiles "by the waters of Babylon" did keep their vow never to forget Jerusalem (Ps. 137). The prophet Ezekiel had warned repeatedly of Jerusalem's imminent doom because of her sins. But once the city had fallen this prophetic watchman turned to hope: in his own good time their God, the good shepherd, would rescue his flock from all places where they had been scattered and would bring them into their own land (Ezek. 34:11-13). The "whole house of Israel," now scattered like dry bones, would once again have life, stand up, and by a miracle of God's grace be brought home into the land of Israel (Ezek. 37:1-14).

And the greatest prophet of all saw visions of a dawning new day. He who proclaimed the dreams familiar to many in the language of Handel's *Messiah* is called Second Isaiah because this unnamed prophet's message is attached to the book of the great eighth-century Isaiah of Jerusalem as his spiritual successor (Isa. 35; 40–55). In a new exodus God himself and his people would return marching on a glorious new highway back to Jerusalem, Zion, city of our God (chaps. 35; 40). And the newly rebuilt nation would have a destiny beyond nationalism. The new Israel—or one to come who epitomizes Israel—would be truly God's servant about whom, declares the Lord of the universe,

I will give you as a light to the nations,
that my salvation may reach to the end of the earth. (49:6)

113

And how was this magnificent dream to come into reality? By the might of a new conqueror, Cyrus, architect of the dawning Persian Empire. Already from his native land (modern Iran) this new world-conqueror had moved with his armies across the north as far as the Aegean Sea in the west. He is unwittingly God's "shepherd," God's "anointed" or "Messiah" (44:28; 45:1)—the only Old Testament reference to a non-Israelite "Messiah." His conquests are preparing the way for a Persian peace (cf. the Pax Romana of Jesus' and Paul's day) which will make possible world evangelization for Yahweh, the Creator, the Savior, the one and only God of the universe (45:5-6, 22-23).

What a glorious vision—the highpoint of the Old Testament! The fact is that this Cyrus, as he testifies in his record known as the Cyrus Cylinder, had a policy of religious and political liberty that was remarkable for his day. For his purposes it was enlightened imperialism to keep subject peoples happy in his far-flung empire, which was eventually to spread from the borders of India in the east, beyond Egypt to North Africa in the west. Let those who had been deported return to their native lands. Let them worship their own gods. Just let them be sure to pay their assessed tribute to the Persian government and obey their governing Persian satraps. With such a proven policy Cyrus actually "liberated" Babylon, to use modern terminology, for he took this longtime enemy capital in 539 B.C. without a battle.

And in the following year, 538 according to the biblical records, Cyrus issued a decree permitting and promoting the return of exiles from Babylon to Jerusalem (Ezra 1:1-11; 6:1-5). Thus ended the sixty-year Babylonian exile.

114

The possibility of a new day had come. A new Jerusalem could spring up phoenixlike from the ashes of the old. But what actually happened?

Evidently a delegation from Babylon did return to Jerusalem, led by a certain Shesh-bazzar (Ezra 1:11; 5:14-16). This man, named governor by the Persian officials, was the son of Jehoiachin, the king of Judah who had been taken captive in 597 and had been released from his Babylonian prison thirty-seven years later (II Kings 24:8-16; 25:27-30). Hence Shesh-bazzar presumably could have reestablished the Davidic royal line in Jerusalem. But did he do so? And how many Jewish exiles returned with him or in the immediately succeeding years? And what was the status of the new Judean community?

Unfortunately such questions as these cannot be answered adequately, for neither biblical nor archaeological sources are available. We no longer have such a running account as the books of Samuel and Kings have provided for the preexilic centuries. And the accounts in Ezra and its parallel in the apocryphal book of I Esdras are fragmentary and disjointed. Actually only two clear shafts of biblical light shine upon the history of the whole two-hundred-year Persian period. These are, respectively, the prophetic books of Haggai and Zechariah and the memoirs of Nehemiah.

Apparently soon after the exiles' return to Jerusalem in 538 B.C. the rebuilding of the temple was begun. Scarcely had the foundations been laid, however, than the work stopped. This stoppage was probably due to two sources of antagonism. One was the quarrel between the enthusiastic Jewish returnees and the dispirited natives who had never left Palestine and regarded the returned exiles as intruders. The other impediment was the opposition

115

from northerners from Samaria, who had been regarded by Judeans as really apostates from Yahweh ever since the days of Jeroboam I's golden calf images.

It was nearly twenty years later (520–518 B.C.) that Haggai and Zechariah challenged the people to rebuild the temple, and the job was completed in March, 515. Unquestionably through all the intervening years since the destruction of Solomon's temple the faithful few had continued to worship in the barren temple area. Now the national sacrificial worship could be resumed, and there was great rejoicing.

But these were not the good old days. The Persian government was now headed by Darius I, who founded the city of Persepolis and left the famous inscription on the cliff wall at Behistun, near Ecbatana. This monarch had supported and financed the rebuilding of the temple in Jerusalem, and prayers were offered regularly in the temple worship for the Persian king (Ezra 6:10).

The province of Judah was governed locally by a dual rulership, similar to that proposed in the plan for the ideal temple and nation in the book of Ezekiel (chaps. 40–48). The high priest Joshua of the line of Zadok was the supreme religious official. Coordinate with him as temporal ruler was King Jehoiachin's grandson with the interesting name of Zerubbabel, "seed of Babylon," governor of the province. Clearly both Haggai and Zechariah pinned their hopes on Zerubbabel's being not simply governor, but the Messiah to inaugurate the dawning new age (Hag. 2:20-23; Zech. 4:1-14; 6:9-15).

And what happened? Did Zerubbabel, not content with being simply a governor owing allegiance to the Persian crown, attempt to ascend David's royal throne? Was he then deposed and perhaps even done away with because

116

of "premature messianic hopes"? No one knows. He simply disappeared from any known records.

In any case, the reality of little Judah's situation was evidently a far cry from the dream of the restoration of a mighty Davidic empire. The picture of the political, economic, and social situation in postexilic Jerusalem which underlies Haggai, Zechariah 1–8, Malachi, and Isaiah 56–66 is not very promising. It is estimated that the total population of Judah was less than half that of the preexilic state, perhaps about twenty thousand soon after the return and no more than fifty thousand a century later.[2]

It was Nehemiah and Ezra who gave significant meaning to the life of the community and set the stage for Judaism's survival to the present day.

The story of Nehemiah, a high official in the Persian government of Artaxerxes I, is vividly told in his own memoirs (Neh. 1:1–7:5). He was one of the most important and influential persons in the Old Testament. Upon hearing firsthand of the distressing situation of his fellow Jews in faraway Jerusalem, he secured funds from Persian sources, went to Jerusalem as governor of Judah in 445 B.C., and personally supervised the reconstruction of the walls and the gates of the city, and even of the morale of the community, in a phenomenally short time. That he was able to do so was due in large measure to the loyalty he elicited from the Jerusalem Jews by his own self-sacrificing devotion.

Most instructive for our purposes is a recounting of the formidable opposition Nehemiah had to overcome in order to achieve his objectives. Besides opposition from within, due to greedy profiteers among the local Jewish citizens, opposition from without came from the four points of the compass. To the west were the Ashdodites,

117

descendants of the Philistines, Israel's perennial foes. To the south were the Idumeans, former Edomites displaced from their homeland south of the Dead Sea, whose forefathers, according to the prophet Obadiah, had gleefully despoiled what was left of Jerusalem and Judah after the destruction of 586 B.C.[3] To the east were the Ammonites from across the Jordan, led by Tobiah from their capital Rabbah of the Ammonites (modern Amman)—and Nehemiah was scandalized to find that during his absence Tobiah was even given quarters in the Jerusalem temple area! But most important of all was the opposition from the Samaritans to the north. These mixed-blood descendants of the colonists imported by the Assyrians after the fall of Samaria who had intermarried with the remnants of the "lost ten tribes of Israel" were led by one Sanballat, who himself subsequently intermarried with the Jerusalem high-priestly family.

That Sanballat was governor of the province of Samaria we know from the Aramaic papyri from the important contemporary colony of Jews in Egypt at Elephantine, at the first cataract of the Nile (near modern Aswan). These Diaspora Jews had built a local temple to Yahweh at which a syncretistic type of worship was carried on. Nevertheless, they were eager to maintain their loyalty to the center of their faith in Jerusalem. So, similarly, the Samaritans insisted upon their loyalty to Yahweh. Eventually, however, these Samaritans built a rival to the Jerusalem temple on Mount Gerizim—and to this day the few hundred Samaritan descendants regard themselves as the true Jews and gather annually for their Passover ceremonies on their sacred mountain.

For Nehemiah—and for Ezra the priest, newly come from Babylonia in essentially the same period[4]—the

118

struggle was for purity of faith and action, for faithfulness to the religion of the fathers. Hence the demand for keeping the Sabbath, for adherence to the rite of circumcision, for divorce from foreign wives, for refusal to permit any taint of exteriorly caused contamination. The new Judaism was so precious that only good Jews should inhabit Jerusalem lest this new jewel be tarnished by foreign contamination.[5]

Whereas Nehemiah provided the political stability for the new state, the priest Ezra, "scribe of the law of the God of heaven" (Ezra 7:12), laid the foundations for the reorganization of the Jewish community on the basis of Torah, the instruction from God. Whether in the famous scene of the reading of the Law to the assembled congregation in Jerusalem (Neh. 8) Ezra was reading only the priestly document or the whole Pentateuch, the so-called Five Books of Moses,[6] is uncertain. What is certain is that from that time on "Israel's transition from a nation to a law community had been made. As such she would thenceforth exist, and this she could do without statehood and even though scattered all over the world. The distinguishing mark of a Jew would not be political nationality, nor primarily ethnic background, nor even regular participation in the Temple cult (impossible for Jews of the Diaspora), but adherence to the law of Moses. The great watershed of Israel's history had been crossed, and her future secured for all time to come."[7]

2. The Jews Under the Greeks

The form of religion known as Judaism, established in the days of Ezra in the Persian period, was to become a significant world faith, but in the next period of Palestine's history it was destined to undergo a profound transformation and to endure terrible testing, when for the first time in this land East and West really met.[8] That meeting was the result of the fabulous military conquests of Alexander the Great of Macedon (336–323 B.C.). Before his untimely death at the age of thirty-two, this youthful Greek master conqueror had already swept through the known world to the borders of India and is said to have stood weeping on the banks of the Indus because there were no more worlds left to conquer.

Far more important than military conquests, however, was the cultural one, for it was the Greek, the Hellenic, dream that there should be one world, a world bound together by Greek culture. That dream was symbolized, and to some extent became reality, in the many urban centers throughout the Middle East which were to carry such Greek names as Antioch, Seleucia, Ptolemaïs, and Philadelphia. In fact, it was in the important Greek coastal city in Egypt, Alexandria, where there was soon a colony of a quarter of a million Jews, that the oldest Greek translation of the Hebrew Scriptures, the Septuagint, was begun in about 250 B.C.

The details of the partition of the Greek-controlled empire among Alexander's generals Antigonus, Ptolemy, and Seleucus need not detain us. Suffice it to say that for approximately 125 years after Alexander's death, until 198 B.C., Palestine was under the control of the Ptolemies, the successors of Ptolemy I, ruling from their capital, Alexandria in Egypt. As one of the most important cities in the world, Alexandria became a center of world Jewry.

As for the governance of the Holy Land itself, the Ptolemies, like the Persians before them, were quite tolerant of the Jews' local religious life and customs, just as long as these subjects paid their taxes to the empire. In fact, there was not even a royal governor in Jerusalem, and the administration of Judea, as the province was called, was in the hands of the high-priestly family and a council of elders.

In the meantime the Seleucid Empire, composed of Asia Minor, Syria, Mesopotamia, and the East, was ruled from its capital, Antioch in Syria. The Seleucid rulers felt that the Ptolemies had stolen Palestine from them, and there were occasional battles between the Ptolemaic and the Seleucid armies in Palestine through these decades. Finally, in 198 B.C., in a battle near the Jordan headwaters on the slopes of Mount Hermon, the Seleucid Antiochus III, the Great, decisively defeated the Egyptian army and annexed Palestine. At first the new ruler was extremely lenient. He even exempted the elders and priests from taxes, and, as Jerusalem was in an economic crisis, he remitted the taxes of the city's inhabitants for three years. All too soon, however, the Jews were to find their Seleucid rulers imposing Greek culture and customs with an iron hand.

In fact, the very rapid spread of Greek, or Hellenic, culture was causing a serious rift in the life of the Jews. Greek had become the language of everyday life everywhere among Jews of the Dispersion. Outside Palestine, Greek and Oriental architecture, and Greek and Oriental cults and mystery religions, were being fused. And inside Palestine the "up-to-date" upper-class Jews, forerunners of the Jewish party later called the Sadducees, insisted that young Jews adopt Greek manners, fashions of dress, and sports, and that gymnasiums, stadiums, and theaters be built. Since such activities inevitably involved

121

some degree of recognition of Greek gods, conservative Jews were scandalized. They feared contamination and the complete breakdown of their unique religious faith and way of life.[9]

It must be emphasized that Judaism's distinctive characteristic was and is its devotion to the law—to Torah, God's instruction to his peculiar people. From the days of Ezra on, this law has been thought of as being embodied especially in the written form in the completed Pentateuch, the so-called Five Books of Moses. These books portray God's revelation of himself both in his historical dealings with his people and in his giving of the law to Moses. This covenant law, the guide to life and morals, was now, in the Seleucid period, interpreted not so much by the priest in temple ritual as, increasingly, by specialists called scribes, who were trained interpreters of the law. The ideal was that of being a holy people, for whom righteousness was to keep the law, and, hence, to be unspotted by the outside world.

Such concentration upon and, indeed, absolutizing of the law created a real problem in the relationship of the Jewish community to non-Jews (Gentiles). To what extent was and is Judaism exclusive, separatist? To what extent universal? As we have seen, there was in Judaism a considerable tradition of universal concern. The call of Abraham was understood as being not simply that Israel should become "a great nation," but that "all the families of the earth shall bless themselves" or be blessed (Gen. 12:2-3). Such universalism was emphasized in Second Isaiah, in the books of Ruth and Jonah, in other passages in the Prophets, and in many of the Psalms, Judaism's hymnbook. The wisdom movement was international in its flavor: Proverbs with its definitions of wisdom and its

122

concern for the good life, Ecclesiastes with its skeptical questioning of orthodox beliefs, Job with its inquiry into God's justice in his dealings with human life and suffering. And all these varied books were on their way to becoming part of the Jewish canon of Scripture, either in the Nebi'im, the Prophets, or the Kethubim, the Writings. They were secondary to the Pentateuch (the Torah, the Law), but they too illumined God's will.

Inevitably, however, the dominant mood of Judaism was one of separatism. The outside pressures on the fragile little community, as we have seen in the Persian period, were too strong for official Judaism to have reacted otherwise. The book of Esther may reflect anti-Jewish persecution in the Persian period. In any case this beautifully told short story and its very popular feast of Purim underline Judaism's sense of outrage—and revenge—at vicious persecution. That persecution came to a climax in the reign of Antiochus IV (175–163 B.C.), known as Antiochus Epiphanes, "god manifest," because he claimed to be Zeus in human form and was so portrayed on coins of the realm.

In biblical language this Antiochus was "a contemptible person to whom royal majesty has not been given" (Dan. 11:21), for he had come to power by assassinating his brother Seleucus IV, the rightful heir to the Seleucid throne of their father, Antiochus III. It was financial troubles which first precipitated struggles in Jerusalem between certain Jews and this new ruler. To pay for the high cost of running the Seleucid Empire, Antiochus imposed higher taxes, and, much to the disgust of the "pious" or "loyal" Jewish party, the Hasidim, forerunners of the Pharisees, he even bartered the sacred high-priestly office to the highest bidder. This was one Jason, who

123

preferred this Greek name to his Jewish name, Joshua. He was brother of the legitimate high priest, Onias III. This new quisling high priest had a Greek gymnasium built in Jerusalem in honor of Antiochus, and soon the resulting corporation of hellenized Jews was indulging in sports honoring the Greek god Heracles.

Only three years later, however, Antiochus again sold the high priesthood to an even higher bidder, one Menelaus, possibly not even of priestly lineage. When subsequently riots broke out in Jerusalem between supporters of these rival priests, Jason and Menelaus, Antiochus took advantage of the situation by marching into Jerusalem with his army. There he killed a number of Jews and plundered the temple, taking its sacred furnishings and even stripping the gold leaf from its facade.

These troubles in the holy city were bad enough. But later Antiochus evidently determined to destroy the religion of Judaism and so carry out Daniel's dire prediction that "the king shall do according to his will; he shall exalt himself and magnify himself above every god, and shall speak astonishing things against the God of gods" (Dan. 11:36). He established in Jerusalem a citadel called the Acra and installed a Seleucid military garrison there. This citadel was to be a Greek polis, the legal substitute for the city of Jerusalem. Hence the temple was to become simply the shrine of a cult in which Yahweh would be identified with Zeus. Therefore in place of the altar for burnt offerings in the temple court an altar to Zeus, "the abomination that makes desolate" (Dan. 11:31; 12:11), was set up, and, as crowning desecration of the temple, the flesh of that most unclean animal of all, the pig, was sacrificed on the high altar. Furthermore it was decreed, not only that there should be pagan altars throughout the land, but also that mothers who circumcised their children should be sentenced to death, no one should observe the Sabbath, and all copies of the Torah should be burned, for the possession of a copy of the Torah was to be a capital offense.

Thus was the unique religion of Judaism to be eliminated. And, sad to relate, hellenized Jews apparently approved, or at least acquiesced in, these measures to modernize the faith of their fathers by bringing it into harmony with universal Greek religion and culture. In fact, some Jews welcomed the assimilation of Yahweh to Zeus, the highest god of paganism. So, it would seem, more than a century and a half of Greek rule in Palestine was to end in the collapse of the unique Jewish faith and life. The West had conquered the East!

3. An Interlude of Freedom: The Maccabean Age

Under these ominous circumstances who could have dreamed that an elderly priest in the village of Modein, a hill town a few miles northwest of Jerusalem, could strike a spark which would result in a period of freedom for the Jews second only to the days of David and Solomon, and lasting for a hundred years? Outraged at the order of Antiochus' Syrian officer that he, the village priest, should offer sacrifice to a pagan god, old Mattathias flatly refused. When a disloyal Jew stepped forward to obey the command, Mattathias killed both the compliant Jew and the commanding officer. Then, calling for all Jews loyal to Yahweh to follow him, he and his five sons, John, Simon, Judas, Eleazer, and Jonathan, fled to the hills.

125

At once these men and their loyal followers began guerilla warfare thoughout the countryside against both Seleucid foreigners and Jews who sided with them. With fanatic zeal they destroyed pagan altars and forcibly circumcised any uncircumcised Jewish children. Seven days a week they were at their task, for in self-defense they suspended the law of the Sabbath.

Old Mattathias soon died, and his third son, Judas, assumed the leadership, winning the nickname "Maccabeus," "the hammer," by his relentless pounding away at the enemy. In fact, the Maccabean war, as it came to be called, soon turned into an out-and-out struggle for independence from Greek control. And, surprisingly, although seriously outnumbered, Judas four times defeated Antiochus' forces in pitched battles. Finally, the Seleucid army was no longer able to cope with this Palestinian revolution—in part because Antiochus was busy in campaigns against the Parthians to the east—and Judas marched triumphantly into Jerusalem.

Judas Maccabeus captured all of the Holy City except the citadel, the Acra; he cleansed the temple, tore down its pagan altar, and restored daily Jewish sacrificial worship. This joyous occasion was December 25, 165 B.C.,[10] when, as it were, the lights went on again. From that day to this the event has been celebrated in the festival of Hanukkah ("Dedication"), the Feast of Lights. Exactly three years previously the desecration of the temple by Antiochus had taken place. Now true Judaism was restored, and the Jewish struggle for complete independence from the Greeks was well on its way.

The fascinating story of this whole struggle for freedom is told in the First and Second Books of the Maccabees. These books were not in the Hebrew Bible, but they were included in the Roman Catholic canon and in the Protestant Apocrypha. First Maccabees is a very reliable source of our knowledge of this period of history to 104 B.C. Second Maccabees is a somewhat more fanciful account.

What may properly be regarded as the manifesto of the heroes of this Maccabean revolution is the biblical book of Daniel. The first half of this, the last of the Old Testament books (Dan. 1–6), is composed of stories of how God rewarded unflinching faithfulness to Yahweh and to Jewish customs in the face of insurmountable odds—the three youths in Nebuchadnezzar's fiery furnace, Daniel in the lions' den. The second half of the book (chaps. 7–12) is outstanding Old Testament apocalyptic, or "revelation," literature. In apocalyptic God is seen as "revealing" historical events by means of visions. Here the history of four successive empires—Babylonian, Median, Persian, and Greek—passes in review. Finally, in a crescendo of historical detail, and as a climax, the visions end with the story of the overthrow of one who is obviously the "contemptible" Antiochus Epiphanes (7:8-28; 8:9-26; 11:21-45). Clearly this book was intended to, and doubtless did, provide the theological assurance to the outnumbered Maccabees, the entire faithful Hasidim, that their seemingly hopeless cause would not be in vain. Their God was on their side! And they were victorious!

One important aspect of this apocalyptic literature and of apocalyptic thinking must be noted. Apocalypticism arises from despair that mere human effort, no matter how herculean, can ever bring about any real social change, can ever really transform bad times into good. Only God's dramatic and sudden intervention in history can do that. The times are in his hands, not ours. Therefore, the

127

faithful, against whatever odds, must stand firmly on God's side to be ready at any moment for that glorious "day of the Lord." Hence the imminent overthrow of Antiochus Epiphanes and his evil regime was shortly to mean the coming of the kingdom of God on earth—now!

Herein lies much of the meaning of the messianic hope in these Old Testament days. It was the firm conviction of many biblical writers that the God who brought his people out of Egypt was the God who would see to it that their history—and all history—would come to a glorious climax: "the day of the Lord," the final consummation when all evil world powers would be overthrown, when God's kingdom would come on earth as in heaven. This would be the Messianic Age. This would be that end-time, that eschaton, when, as seen in the two visions which provide the basic framework for Daniel's apocalyptic (chaps. 2 and 7) "the God of heaven will set up a kingdom which shall never be destroyed, nor shall its sovereignty be left to another people" (2:44), "and the kingdom and the dominion / and the greatness of the kingdoms under the whole heaven / shall be given to the people of the saints of the Most High; / their kingdom shall be an everlasting kingdom, / and all dominions shall serve and obey them" (7:27). Interestingly enough, in this book of Daniel and in the victorious Maccabean restoration of the temple worship celebrated by Hanukkah, there was no one Messiah, no royal messianic figure. Unlike Zerubbabel in the earlier days of Haggai and Zechariah, the conquering Judas Maccabeus was not considered the Messiah-to-be.[11] However, this remarkable victory of the Hasidim over the pagans must surely have been interpreted as ushering in the kingdom of God on earth.[12]

The inauguration of the Maccabean Age with Judas'

phenomenal recapture of Jerusalem and Judea from its pagan overlords was not the beginning of the Messianic Age. But it was the inauguration of an unprecedented era of Jewish self-government and independence reminiscent of the kingdom of David and Solomon.

As we have seen, in 165 B.C. Judas had wrested all of Judea except the Acra in Jerusalem from the foreign overlords, and in his peace with the Syrian regent he obtained complete freedom of worship for the Jews. Subsequently he was able to defend Judea from attempts to regain Jerusalem.

Upon Judas' untimely death in battle in 161 B.C., his brother Jonathan took over the leadership and cleverly maneuvered for favor among rival claimants to the Seleucid throne. Thus Jonathan was appointed high priest and, in the view of some of the Jews, soiled his sacred office by his role as military and political leader. According to some historians it was this Jonathan who really initiated the rule of the Maccabean house, which was to continue for nearly a century.

Jonathan was assassinated through Seleucid political intrigue in 143 B.C., and Simon, the third son of Mattathias, succeeded his brother as high priest and popular military leader. He was able to eliminate the last vestige of foreign rule by capturing the Acra and expelling its pagan inhabitants. Furthermore, with the acclaim of his own people Simon was made hereditary high priest and ethnarch (governor) by a decree recorded on a tablet placed in the temple. Thus began officially the rule of the house of the Hasmoneans, which was the family name of Mattathias and his descendants. As we have seen, "Maccabee" was only a nickname of Judas. Although Simon was in power for less than a decade, he has been adjudged to be "perhaps the best ruler the Jews ever had in the postexilic period, though he was not their king." [13] A man of integrity and a wise and just administrator, Simon presided over an era of peace in which attention was paid to literature and the arts, to trade and farming. Seemingly with this third son of Mattathias the revolutionary, a new age had dawned.

After the assassination of Simon in 134 B.C., his son John Hyrcanus ruled for thirty years as the first priest-king of the Hasmoneans (whether he ever actually took the title of king is a disputed point, however). During his reign he extended the borders of Judea to include Idumea in the south, the Galilee region in the north, and some of Transjordan in the east—thus virtually restoring the boundaries of the previous combined kingdoms of Israel and Judah. In these years Jewish independence was such that it was almost as if the old Davidic royal house had been restored in extent, but not in fact, for the Hasmoneans were not descendants of the royal line.

Nevertheless, perhaps not unlike the situation in the latter days of David's reign, the struggles within these borders were often fierce. In the south the Idumeans, descendants of the Hebrews' ancient rivals the Edomites, were forced to accept circumcision and become Jews, even though the Jews never were to consider the Idumeans as anything but half-pagan Edomites. In the north Hyrcanus incurred the everlasting wrath of the Samaritans by destroying Samaria, Shechem, and, above all, their holy temple on Mount Gerizim.

In addition to these unhappy circumstances, the rivalry within the country between the two growing and strong religio-political parties, the Pharisees and the Sadducees, became severe. The more popular party, the Pharisees, spiritual descendants of the Hasidim, were separatists, zealous for keeping the Torah, and very leery of contamination from Greek culture. The Sadducees, the priestly and politically minded aristocracy, were ready to adjust to Hellenic culture in folk customs and everyday life.

Strikingly enough, these two parties reversed their positions in their handling of the Torah, the Pentateuch. The otherwise assimilationist Sadducees affirmed only the Torah and its prescriptions as binding on life and thought. Hence they rejected such doctrines as the resurrection of the body and the hope of a future life which are not clearly set forth in the Torah. On the other hand, the Pharisees, very rigid in their observance of the customs of the Torah—dietary regulations, circumcision, fasting, prayer—accepted the teachings of that part of the canon of Scripture called the Prophets, the Nebi'im. Also, in order to adapt the Torah to the changing conditions of life, they developed a body of oral law called "the tradition of the elders." This oral law was in subsequent centuries incorporated in the Mishnah and the Talmud.

When for political advantage John Hyrcanus turned from his family's Pharisaic upbringing to become a Hellenistic Sadducean sympathizer—even changing his sons' names from Judas, Mattathias, and Jonathan to Aristobulus, Antigonus, and Alexander Janneus—terrific antagonism was aroused in the land. Nevertheless the thirty-year reign of John Hyrcanus, which ended with his death in 104 B.C., was the high point of the period of Jewish independence under the Hasmoneans.

It is probable that during John Hyrcanus' reign the covenant community at Qumran in the Judean desert some twelve miles south of Jericho, now world famous for its library known as the Dead Sea Scrolls, was founded. A

131

group of devout Jews, outraged at the worldliness of the priestly ruling class in Jerusalem, fled to this isolated region to establish a community completely separated from the world. There they practiced a monastic type of life, awaiting the coming of God's kingdom which would follow the final "war of the Sons of Light against the Sons of Darkness" of this world. Over against the priest-kings of this age, the kingdom to come would be inaugurated by two messianic figures, one from the royal line of David, the other from the priestly tribe of Levi. This community was probably related to the sect called the Essenes. It was to have close affinities with the style of life and the message of John the Baptist, and its influence, at least indirectly, on Jesus and early Christianity is noteworthy.

After the reign of John Hyrcanus ended in 104 B.C., much of the final forty-one years of Jewish independence under the Hasmoneans was marked by internal strife. John Hyrcanus' second son, Alexander Janneus, in a reign of more than a quarter of a century, enlarged the boundaries of the country to include almost all of the ancient kingdom of David. When Janneus died in battle in Transjordan, he was succeeded by his widow, Salome Alexandra, who had previously been his elder brother's wife also. Largely because under her rule the Pharisees controlled the country internally, her reign was a nine-year period of peace. The elder of her sons, Hyrcanus II, she made high priest; the younger, Aristobulus II, she named the political ruler. Thus once again the religious and the political ruling authority were divided.

It was the squabble between these two brothers, prompted in part by the underlying antipathy between the Pharisees and the Sadducees and fostered by the Nabatean Arabians, that led the Roman commander-in-chief Pompey to agree to settle the Jews' internal arguments. This Pompey did by marching on Jerusalem in 63 B.C. A terrible massacre of twelve thousand Jews followed. Priests were killed at the altar. Roman cohorts even entered the holy of holies. Nevertheless, the temple was not plundered, and Jewish sacrificial worship was ordered resumed. But, largely because of the continuous internal strife in the Jewish community and stupid appeals by the various parties for Roman help, the Jews brought their independence crashing down on their heads. Rome took over!

Despite the tragic end of this period of Jewish freedom, we must not underestimate the significance of this century. As might be expected, under the subsequent Roman domination the hope was always alive, spurred on especially by such vigorous political revolutionary parties as the Zealots, that Maccabean independence could be restored. Even more important, the religion of Judaism, especially as fostered by the Pharisees, was firmly established. The tremendous scribal activity of studying, copying, reading, and teaching the Law and the Prophets (reflected in the Dead Sea Scrolls) was to continue throughout the generations. It has been said that "all the foundation stones of modern Jewry were well and truly laid during the period of Hasmonean rule." [14]

4. The Jews Under the Romans

Approximately two hundred years remain of our biblical story. This was the Roman period, from Pompey's conquest of Palestine in 63 B.C. until the second and final Jewish revolt in A.D. 132–34.

In the first quarter of a century after Pompey brought

133

Palestine under Roman rule by conquering Jerusalem, the Maccabean dynasty slowly came to its end. This took place in a struggle for political power primarily with an Idumean—Antipater, father of Herod the Great. When Julius Caesar became absolute Roman ruler in 48 B.C., he appointed Antipater governor of Palestine. The last Hasmonean to rule, Antigonus, was defeated by Herod in 37 B.C., and although Antigonus had surrendered unconditionally, he was beheaded at Antioch by the Romans. Three years earlier the Roman Senate had proclaimed Herod king of the Jews. Now he could establish himself as king.

The thirty-three-year reign of Herod the Great was a period of both prosperous building enterprises and puzzling, ruthless intrigue. This Idumean ruler was a Jew only by birth, not a convert. He had previously been governor of the Galilee region, and Mariamne of the Maccabean family was one of his ten wives. He rebuilt much of Jerusalem. He built the great cities of Sebaste, formerly Samaria, and the seaport Caesarea, both in honor of the Roman emperor Augustus. He enlarged and refortified the fortress-palace of Masada, the remarkable citadel overlooking the Dead Sea which is renowned through recent excavations, and built or rebuilt many other fortresses. He solved Jerusalem's water supply problem by an aqueduct from two springs south of Bethlehem. His enlarging and rebuilding of the temple complex produced famous and beautiful structures which were doubtless more glorious than the original temple built by Solomon.

Despite all this the Jews continued to hate him. His heavy taxation policies and his tyranny were grievous. He insisted on interfering in the high priesthood's affairs, and he held in contempt the Sanhedrin, the high court of

Judaism on which sat such famous teachers as Shammai and Hillel.

According to New Testament accounts Jesus was born in one of the latter years of Herod's reign and barely escaped the brutality of his slaughter of the innocents (Matt. 2:1-18; Luke 2:1-7). With similar inhumanity Herod slew Maccabean members of his family: his mother-in-law, his wife Mariamne, and his own children by her. No wonder that when he died in 4 B.C. Jewish leaders requested Rome to end the rule of the Herodians.

Rome's response, however, was to divide Palestine into three regions to be ruled over by members of Herod's family. By far the largest region, Judea, Idumea, and Samaria, was ruled by Herod's son Archelaus as ethnarch. While his rule was begun with kindliness to the Jews, before ten years had passed both Jews and Samaritans complained so loudly to Rome of Archelaus' brutal treatment that he was banished to Gaul in A.D. 6. Henceforth his territory, formerly kingdom, was reduced to a province of the Roman Empire, and in the next sixty years it was ruled by a succession of fourteen prefects, later called procurators, except for a three-year interval of kingship under Agrippa I.

The procurators normally resided at the capital, Caesarea, on the Mediterranean Sea. The most famous of these often cruel and usually hated rulers of the Jews is Pontius Pilate, whose ten-year rule was from A.D. 26 to 36. On the whole the procurators respected Jewish religious scruples. Internal administration of Jewish affairs was given over to the Sanhedrin, while the procurator was responsible for taxation and maintaining public order. To the procurator was reserved the right to pass death sentences, the most famous being that of Pontius Pilate by which Jesus was crucified, perhaps on Friday, April 7, A.D. 30.[15]

For forty-three years, from 4 B.C. to A.D. 39, another son of Herod, Herod Antipas, whom Jesus called "that fox" (Luke 13:32), ruled as tetrarch over Galilee and the Transjordan area called Perea. He is perhaps best known for the founding of the city of Tiberias, named for the Roman emperor, on the western shore of the Sea of Galilee, and the beheading of John the Baptist (Matt. 14:1-12; Mark 6:17-29; Luke 3:19-20).

The third area ruled by a son of Herod was the northern Transjordan territory southeast of Mount Hermon. Here from 4 B.C. to A.D. 34 Herod Philip ruled as tetrarch. He rebuilt and enlarged the city with the distinctive name of Caesarea Philippi (modern Banias).

For a brief period the country was once again united under Herod the Great's grandson, Herod Agrippa I. Agrippa was given Herod Philip's territory in A.D. 37 and the title of king by the Roman emperor Caligula. In 39 he was given Herod Antipas' Galilee and Perea, and in 41 he replaced the procurators as governor of Judea. Agrippa won some support from the Pharisees. He took measures to please Jews in both Jerusalem and Alexandria. He was reported as persecuting the growing Christian church, as he killed James the son of Zebedee and arrested Peter (Acts 12:1-3). He died, some think of venereal disease, soon after the people hailed him as a god in 44 (Acts 12:20-23).

In the years after the death of Herod Agrippa I, a revolutionary mood swept the country. There were repeated riots and attempts at rebellion against the ruling Romans. In the Galilee region the authorities constantly had to contend with bands of Jewish malcontents and outlaws. The Zealots and the Sicarii were two extreme nationalist groups who used terrorist activities in a determined effort to drive the Romans out of the country.[16]

The tension in these years was mounting. Antonius Felix, procurator of Judea from 52 to 60, treacherously used the services of brigands, perhaps the Sicarii, to murder the high priest Jonathan. When the apostle Paul was arrested in the temple area in Jerusalem, he was asked by the local military tribune, "Are you not the Egyptian, then, who recently stirred up a revolt and led the four thousand men of the Assassins out into the wilderness?" (Acts 21:38). Paul was first summoned before this procurator Felix in Caesarea (Acts 23:24–24:27). Then, after two long years in prison, he was brought before Porcius Festus, Felix's successor as procurator, at which time Paul appealed to the emperor himself (Acts 25:1-12).

In the meantime Herod Agrippa II, a lad of eleven when his father Herod Agrippa I died in 44, had become king over the former tetrarchy of Philip and over parts of Galilee, Perea, and Judea. It was on a state ceremonial visit to Festus at Caesarea that Herod Agrippa II and Festus agreed, after hearing Paul's magnificent speech of defense, that "this man could have been set free if he had not appealed to Caesar" (Acts 26:32). While King Agrippa seemed to understand Jewish concerns, he always sided with the Romans. His sister Berenice—with whom he had an incestuous relationship that caused no little stir—is said to have become the mistress of Titus, who destroyed Jerusalem in 70.

Finally, when in May, 66, the procurator Gessius Florus violated the temple treasury and allowed Roman troops to murder and plunder in Jerusalem, the Jewish revolt broke out in earnest. Though most Pharisees and Sadducees had preferred peace, rebellion now spread throughout the land. The famous Jewish historian Flavius Josephus was in charge of Jewish forces in the Galilee region, but he surrendered to the Romans the following year.

At first the Jews were successful in their revolt, although in 68 the Qumran community was destroyed by Roman troops. The Zealots controlled the city of Jerusalem and the fortresses which had been constructed by Herod the Great at Herodium, a few miles south of Jerusalem, and at Masada, far to the south on the shore of the Dead Sea.

The Roman general Vespasian besieged Jerusalem in 69, and when, later that year, he was made emperor, his son Titus took over. In July, 70, Titus entered Jerusalem, and the following month he set fire to the temple and razed the city, carrying off temple treasures in triumph for display in Rome—the table of shewbread, the golden lampstand, a scroll of the Law. In 71 he erected a triumphal arch in Rome as a memorial of his successes.

Both Jewish and Roman coins reflect the history of these dramatic years. Only in the fortress of Masada were Jewish rebels able to hold out for three more years, finally committing suicide in 73 rather than surrender to the Romans. Thus in 70 the first Jewish revolt against Rome came to its tragic end. The temple, destroyed for the second time, has never been rebuilt.

In the period of reconstruction after Jerusalem's fall Judaism remained a permitted religion under Roman rule, but the temple worship was gone. Instead Judaism continued primarily as the religion of the written Torah, with its center at Jamnia near the coast. There famous rabbis of the house of Hillel served as a supreme court, interpreting the law and making decisions for the Jewish community. In about 90 a decision was made as to what books could be considered sacred Scripture. The books of the Kethubim, the Writings, were placed alongside, but secondary to, the previously accepted Law and Prophets. Thus the Palestinian Jewish canon was closed.

A second and final Jewish revolt broke out in 132 during the reign of the emperor Hadrian. Presumably this was occasioned by the emperor's plan to rebuild Jerusalem as a Roman colony with a shrine to Jupiter on the site of the destroyed temple. Prohibited acts would include the rite of circumcision.

The leader of the revolt was Simon ben Kozeba—or bar Kochba, "son of the star." Such an illustrious religious leader as Rabbi Akiba strongly backed Simon. Letters from Simon have been found in caves near the Dead Sea. Jerusalem was briefly liberated from Roman rule, and coins celebrating the liberation were minted with the inscription "Simon, Prince of Israel."

But the liberation was short-lived. In 134 Jerusalem was recaptured by the Romans, and Simon made a last stand in a village six miles southwest of the Holy City. The Romans carried out the emperor's plan. Jerusalem was renamed Colonia Aelia Capitolina, and in the temple area was built a shrine dedicated to the god Jupiter (Zeus) and to the emperor Hadrian.

Thus the specifically biblical portion of our story ends. The Jews had been conquered. To this day the worship of ancient Israel on the spot traditionally hallowed by Abraham's near sacrifice of Isaac, and by the centuries of worship at Solomon's temple and its successors, has never been revived. But the Jewish religion has remained gloriously undefeated. Long since spread around the globe, Judaism—and its daughter faith, Christianity—live vibrantly on through the centuries.

Notes

1. The term *Jew* or *Jews* was first used in the Bible in II Kings 25:25, and in Jeremiah 32:12; 34:9; 38:19; 40:11, 12, 15; 41:3; 44:1; 52:28, 30, to refer to the citizens of Judah who were living in or near Jerusalem or who had already fled to neighboring countries in the southern kingdom's last days. In postexilic books, especially Ezra, Nehemiah, and Esther, the term refers either to a subject of the province of Judah or to a member of the Jewish people or religion, or to both.

   The centuries-long debate continues even in the modern state of Israel as to how far *Jew* appropriately designates biological or cultural origin, political allegiance, and/or religious affiliation. In his article "Jew, Jews, Jewess," *The Interpreter's Dictionary of the Bible,* ed. George A. Buttrick (Nashville: Abingdon Press, 1962), vol. 2, p. 898, J. A. Sanders summarizes as follows: "The usage of the term 'Jew' was very fluid even in biblical times. . . . Today the term is even more fluid. There are Jews both by religion and by birth, by religion but not by birth, and by birth but not by religion. Race, nationality, physical type, language, culture, belief—none of these nor any combination of these will distinguish or identify the Jew. While it is without question that the Jews represent a clearly traceable continuum in the history of mankind, there is no least common denominator for the some twelve million people today who call themselves Jews. Indeed, perhaps the best that can be said is that he is a Jew who says he is."

2. W. F. Albright, *The Biblical Period from Abraham to Ezra* (Torchbooks; New York: Harper & Row, 1963), pp. 87, 92-93, 110-11.

3. In Nehemiah's memoirs these southern enemies are called "the Arabs" (Neh. 4:7), and their leader "Geshem the Arab" (Neh. 2:19; 6:1). As noted in chaps. 1–3 of the present volume, the term *Arab* is frequently a general term meaning "nomad." It refers to many and various, often nomadic, people of the East, including Ishmaelites, Midianites, Edomites, and Nabateans, who usually came originally from the northern part of the large peninsula of Arabia. In later biblical material this more general term *Arab* or *Arabs*—

140

which may also be rendered "Arabian" or "Arabians"—
replaces the earlier, more specific tribal designation
Ishmaelite, etc. See Arthur Jeffery, "Arabians," *Interpreter's
Dictionary of the Bible,* vol. 1, pp. 181-84.

"Arabians" were among the many groups present at
Pentecost—the only New Testament reference to these
people (Acts 2:11). In the Old Testament, other than the
three references in Nehemiah mentioned above, *Arab* or
Arabs appears only seven times elsewhere: as the name of a
town in Judah (Josh. 15:52); as a synonym for desert "nomad"
(Isa. 13:20; Jer. 3:2); and as specific enemy tribesmen from
the Edomite region who brought huge tribute of rams and
he-goats to King Jehoshaphat of Judah (II Chron. 17:11),
invaded Judah in subsequent years (II Chron. 21:16-17;
22:1), and finally were defeated in their city of Gurbaal by
King Uzziah of Judah (II Chron. 26:7).

4. Ezra's arrival in Jerusalem from Babylonia was in "the
   seventh year of Artaxerxes" (Ezra 7:7). But whether this
   "seventh year" was 458 B.C. in the reign of Artaxerxes I or
   398 B.C. in the reign of Artaxerxes II, or whether "seventh
   year" is an error for the "thirty-seventh year" of Artaxerxes I
   (428 B.C.) is an unsettled question among biblical scholars.

5. Certain passages in Isaiah 56–66 and the books of Ruth and
   Jonah may have been written to promote universalism in
   order to combat this narrow exclusivism.

6. Note that to this day in Judaism the Torah or Law, five books
   from Genesis through Deuteronomy, constitute the primary
   portion of the Hebrew Bible. The Prophets and the Writings,
   the second and third divisions, are secondary. And, indeed,
   the Samaritans still use only the Torah.

7. John Bright, *A History of Israel,* 2d ed. (Philadelphia: The
   Westminster Press, 1972), p. 392.

8. In some respects the founding of and present existence of
   the state of Israel constitutes a similar period of crisis in the
   Middle East, for in large measure Israel may be seen as a
   primarily Western state set down in the midst of an
   inherently Eastern cultural milieu.

9. Cf. the reactions of the devout Muslim Arab parent in
   present-day Jerusalem. Eastern customs have long prohibit-

ed teen-age sons from even so much as walking hand-in-hand down the street with a girl, although teen-age young men may often be seen holding hands. Now when the Arab father hears of the activities of Western young people around movie houses in West Jerusalem he wonders how he can ever teach his children to be moral—from his perspective!

10. A number of scholars give the date as 164 B.C. Note that because of uncertainty as to the Seleucid method of reckoning the year there are frequent discrepancies in dates in the various histories of this period.

11. Since the Messiah was expected to be of the royal line of David, Judas did not qualify. The "Son of man" concept of the Messiah, that of a supernatural figure coming down from the clouds of heaven, is a later conception. In Daniel 7:13,27, "one like a son of man" is clearly to be interpreted as referring to "the people of the saints of the Most High," possibly led by a messianic king, but not necessarily so.

12. Cf. the ecstasy at the conclusion of the Six Day War in June, 1967, when Arab homes in the former Jewish Quarter near the Wailing Wall in Jerusalem were bulldozed out to make a large plaza. In the expectation of certain orthodox Jews the Messiah would now appear at the Feast of Weeks, Pentecost, only a few days away, and hurried preparations must be made! See Charles Harbutt, "Eyewitness to War in the Holy Land," *National Geographic*, 132, no. 6 (December 1967), pp. 782-95.

13. Nigel Turner, "Hasmoneans," *Interpreter's Dictionary of the Bible*, vol. 2, p. 530.

14. *Ibid.*, p. 535.

15. Gordon B. Duncan, "Chronology," *Interpreter's One-Volume Commentary on the Bible*, pp. 1275, 1282.

16. Cf. the terrorist activities of Jewish underground groups during the last days of the British mandate before 1948. According to some historians, they made governing so unbearable that the British finally gave up.

9

Jerusalem Through Three Millennia

If I forget you, O Jerusalem,
  let my right hand wither!
Let my tongue cleave to the roof of my mouth,
  if I do not remember you,
if I do not set Jerusalem
  above my highest joy!   (Ps. 137:5-6)

So vowed the psalmist exiled from his holy city, as he languished "by the waters of Babylon" in the sixth century B.C. His solemn pledge was born of loyalty to the God whom his fathers had worshiped for centuries at the holy temple in Jerusalem. His love of Jerusalem has been shared by devout persons over three thousand years—and, indeed, by three world faiths, Judaism, Christianity, and Islam. A brief account of these three millennia of Jerusalem's story can illumine present-day loyalties toward and struggles over this sacred site.[1]

1. Jerusalem in Old Testament Times

The story of Jerusalem began far earlier than three thousand years ago. Prehistoric human habitation of the area around Jerusalem goes back to paleolithic times, according to the evidence of flints found in nearby valleys, and pottery from the fourth millennium B.C. has turned up in excavations at Jerusalem itself. During the third and the early second millennium there was on the site a small walled city of some eight or nine acres in size.

The name Jerusalem appears first in Egyptian texts of the nineteenth and eighteenth centuries B.C. According to the biblical account, in this Middle Bronze Age the patriarch Abraham received bread and wine and the blessing of Melchizedek king of Salem (Gen. 14:17-20). This "king of Salem" was a priest of the Canaanite high god El Elyon, "God Most High." Salem was Jerusalem (Ps. 76:2) and is the first name of the city to appear in the Bible.

The word *Jerusalem* means "foundation of Shalem." Quite probably the reference both here and in the earlier Egyptian texts is to a Canaanite god named Shalem. However, the close association of the name with the significant Hebrew word *shalom*, "peace," has naturally led to the common traditional interpretation "the city of peace."

Interestingly enough, the name for Jerusalem associated with Abraham is Moriah, for presumably it was on this "mount" where later Solomon's temple was built that Abraham almost sacrificed his son Isaac (Gen. 22:1-14; II Chron. 3:1).

In the fourteenth century B.C. the city of Jerusalem was the center of one of the many vassal states of Egypt. Its Hurrian ruler, Abdu-Hepa, appealed desperately in his letters (which are among the Amarna Tablets) for Egyptian troops to help him defend his city against invading Habiru.

In the period of the conquest and settlement of Canaan by the Israelites under Joshua, Jerusalem was the city of a relatively unknown Canaanite clan called the Jebusites. Their king with the name Adonizedek, "my lord is righteousness" (cf. Melchizedek, "my king is righteousness," mentioned above) met his death when his coalition of five Amorite kings was crushed by Joshua's forces (Josh. 10:1-14). A later attempt by the tribe of Judah to capture Jerusalem was successful at least in gaining control of the environs of the city (Judg. 1:1-8), but the Jebusites were not driven out of the city (Josh. 15:63; Judg. 1:21). The incoming Israelites' attitude toward the city is indicated in the story of how the Ephraimite Levite refused to spend the night in "the city of foreigners, who do not belong to the people of Israel" (Judg. 19:11-12).

Our concern with the story of Jerusalem really begins with David's capture of it from the Jebusites *ca.* 996 B.C.[2] The method by which David was able to take the fortified city is not altogether clear from the two biblical accounts (II Sam. 5:6-9; I Chron. 11:4-8). Apparently David's commander Joab and his men fought their way up into the city, one by one, by climbing up the water shaft which had been cut through the rock by the Jebusites from within the city walls to the spring of Gihon in the Kidron valley. This daring exploit[3]—a kind of Trojan horse story without a Trojan horse—foiled the Jebusites' boast that their city was so well defended that the blind and the lame would be sufficient human resources to protect it.

Because of David's conquest the name "the city of David" was henceforth given to this "stronghold of Zion."[4] Zion was the triangular eastern hill wedged between the Tyropoeon valley on the west and the Kidron valley on the east. It was located on the long, narrow southern end of the eastern hill called Ophel, south of the present-day Old City of Jerusalem. The broader northern

145

end of Zion was the location where Solomon's temple was later built, now the site of the Muslim Sacred Precinct, or Haram esh-Sherif. Between the original city of David on the south and the temple area on the north was the area called the Millo. The statement that "David built the city round about from the Millo inward" (II Sam. 5:9) probably refers to terracing and building up the area to provide a platform for the palace and other buildings.

David's establishing of his capital at Jerusalem was of strategic and historical significance. This formerly Jebusite city had no previous loyalty to any of the Israelites. It was neither northern nor southern and so could not be claimed either by the Israelite tribal confederacy of the north or by the dominant tribe of Judah in the south. Furthermore, its location was between the north and the south—as it were, on the Mason-Dixon line of ancient Palestine—hence it is sometimes compared to Washington, D.C. Presumably when "all the tribes of Israel came to David at Hebron" and requested him to carry out the Lord's command for him to be "shepherd" and "prince over Israel" (II Sam. 5:1-3), this was the political culmination of a popular movement.

Actually Jerusalem came to be regarded almost as David's own personal possession, "the city of David," a state within a state. Perhaps partly for this reason the dynasty of David, his descendants, ruled in Jerusalem for over four hundred years. And the hope of some form of restoration of his rule by a Messiah from "the house of David" has persisted through the centuries.

Most important was the fact that David made Jerusalem his religious as well as his political capital. This he did by bringing up to Jerusalem the ark, the sacred object of the northern tribes and the symbol of the national God (II

Sam. 6). According to the biblical account, the king, embarrassedly aware of his own palace, wanted to build an appropriate "house of cedar" for the ark instead of leaving it in a tent in Jerusalem (II Sam. 7:1-3). The prophet Nathan, however, in a delightful play on words, told David that he must not build a house for God, but that God would build a house for him, the house of David, an everlasting dynasty (II Sam. 7:4-17).

Perhaps the most widely known fact about ancient Jerusalem is that it was the site of the temple built by David's son and successor, Solomon. The exact location was an extensive platform built around the bedrock threshing floor of Araunah the Jebusite (II Sam. 24:18-35; I Chron. 21:28–22:1).[5] The temple building itself was a rectangle some ninety feet long by thirty feet wide and forty-five feet high. The easternmost of the three rooms was the vestibule or entrance hall, then came the nave or main room, and finally the inner sanctuary, or holy of holies. This last room was a perfect cube of about thirty feet (I Kings 6:2-6, 20). In the holy of holies was housed the ark. The sacrificial worship took place outside the building in the large courtyard. The building itself was famous for its ornate beauty, the product of Phoenician artisanship.

Solomon's reign of luxury included a great complex of buildings located probably in the area to the south between the temple and the city of David. These included a palace, "his own house," the House of the Forest of Lebanon, the Hall of Pillars, the Hall of the Throne, and chapels for his various foreign wives, especially one for Pharaoh's daughter (I Kings 7:1-8; 9:24). But the lasting memory of his reign is his temple, the national center of worship which was to stand for three and three-quarter centuries and was subsequently to provide either successor buildings or haunting desires for such to this present day.

When the kingdom of David and Solomon broke into the two rival kingdoms of Israel and Judah, Jerusalem's preeminence as political and religious capital continued, chiefly because it was the site of the temple. In the various struggles between Judah and her neighbors Jerusalem was often victimized. This happened almost immediately after Judah became a separate state, when, in the reign of Rehoboam, Pharaoh Shishak of Egypt plundered the temple and palace in Jerusalem (I Kings 14:25-28). Later King Jehoash repaired damages done to the temple in the six-year reign of the northern usurper Athaliah, but he had to buy off Hazael king of Syria with treasures from the temple and the palace (II Kings 12:4-18). In the reign of Amaziah the armed forces of the northern kingdom, besides plundering the temple and the palace, even "broke down the wall of Jerusalem for four hundred cubits," about two hundred yards (II Kings 14:13-14), damages which were repaired when Uzziah in his long and successful reign considerably strengthened Jerusalem's fortifications.

The most famous measure taken to defend Jerusalem in Old Testament times was the digging of the Siloam tunnel in the days of King Hezekiah (II Kings 20:20; II Chron. 32:2-3, 30). For centuries the water from the Gihon spring had flowed through an open rock-cut channel around the southern end of the hill of Ophel, but in order to protect the city's water supply during the imminent siege by the Assyrian king Sennacherib in the days of Isaiah, Hezekiah had the long tunnel dug from the spring to the then completely covered and thus camouflaged pool of Siloam.

This extraordinary feat of ancient engineering twists and turns for a quarter of a mile through the solid rock under the city. Two teams of workmen dug the tunnel, beginning at each end and, seemingly miraculously, meeting in the middle. An inscription recording the joy of the teams when they heard the sound of each other's picks as they neared the middle was found on the walls of the tunnel nearly a hundred years ago. And to this day during the dry season visitors trudge through the tunnel and marvel at the marks left by the picks of Hezekiah's diggers in the eighth century B.C., still visible on the walls.

The remarkable deliverance of Jerusalem from Sennacherib's siege has long been celebrated (II Kings 19:32-37; II Chron. 32:20-22; Isa. 37:33-38). During the subsequent reign, lasting more than half a century, of Hezekiah's son Manasseh, when Judah was both religiously and politically dominated by Assyria, Jerusalem's king was permitted to refortify and expand the city to the west and north (II Chron. 33:14). It was under Manasseh's grandson King Josiah that once again true worship of Yahweh was restored in Jerusalem and throughout the land. According to the book of the law found in the temple in 621 B.C., which was probably at least the major portion of our book of Deuteronomy, pagan Assyrian and other idolatrous objects were removed from the temple.

Despite the reform of Josiah, however, the prophets Zephaniah, Jeremiah, and Ezekiel predicted that because of returning and continued apostasy from Yahweh, even in the temple, the disastrous end of Jerusalem and the nation was close at hand. The popular notion that God held his holy city and temple to be inviolable (for, after all, the mighty power of Assyria had failed to take them) was false doctrine. The God who had brought their fathers out of the land of Egypt could and would destroy his people if they repudiated his covenant!

In the rapid turnover of international events in the last days of Judah, Josiah's son Jehoiakim, originally appointed by Egypt, transferred his allegiance to the power of Babylon but soon made the fatal mistake of revolting and died during Nebuchadnezzar's subsequent siege of Jerusalem. After reigning for only three months, Jehoiakim's eighteen-year-old son and successor, Jehoiachin, surrendered to the enemy on March 16, 597 B.C. Some ten thousand leading citizens were carried away to Babylon in this first captivity from Jerusalem, but the city was not destroyed, although the temple and palace were plundered (II Kings 24:1-17). When later, however, Zedekiah also revolted against Babylon, Nebuchadnezzar's revenge was swift and thorough. Even then, from January, 588, to July, 586, the city withstood the Babylonian siege. But finally, after the deportation to Babylon of many more of Jerusalem's citizens, the city was razed.

The resurrection of Jerusalem is one of the glorious miracles of history. As we have seen in the previous chapter (pp. 114-16), after Cyrus' capture of Babylon in 539 B.C., Jewish exiles there were permitted to return to Jerusalem under Shesh-bazzar, and they presumably began to rebuild the city. Some twenty years later in the days of Zerubbabel, and at the urging of the prophets Haggai and Zechariah, the temple was rebuilt. It was completed with great rejoicing in March, 515.

In the middle of the following century, in 445 B.C., the dynamic Jewish high official in the Persian government, Nehemiah, set to work to rebuild the walls of the city. Nehemiah's famous night ride, obviously by the light of the moon, when he surveyed the ruins to the point where "there was no place for the beast that was under [him] to pass" (Neh. 2:14), was followed by a remarkable rebuilding program accomplished, despite great difficulties, in fifty-two days (6:15). The various gates, towers, and portions of the walls mentioned in detail in Nehemiah's memoirs have been variously identified. Some have been confirmed by archaeology, but most have been destroyed by the many subsequent destructions and rebuildings of the city.

With Nehemiah political stability was brought to the newly fortified city. But it must be remembered that in Nehemiah's time the boundaries of the little province of Judah probably extended only about ten miles to the north of Jerusalem and twenty miles to the south and west. The genius of the community of Judaism was and would continue to be, not its political extent, but its devotion, eventually worldwide, to the Torah, the instruction from God, under the impetus of the priest-scribe Ezra. Nevertheless there were frequent visions of the future glory of the city of Jerusalem (Joel 3:11-21; Zech. 14).

Until the conquest of the East by Alexander the Great, Jerusalem had been the capital of a little eastern Mediterranean state located at the western edge of empires centered in western Asia. Actually the city lay on the military and commercial crossroads between the normally dominant Mesopotamian power to the northeast—Assyria and Babylon in the Tigris-Euphrates valley—and its Egyptian rival the southwest. But now, with the Greek conquest of the East, Jerusalem became for a thousand years a city located on the eastern fringe of a great Western empire, governed first by Greeks, and then for seven hundred years, by Romans.

Obviously such a transition within the life of Jerusalem in the Greek period was gradual. From the capture of Jerusalem by Ptolemy I in 320 B.C. until, in 198 B.C., Palestine became a part of the Seleucid Empire, as we have seen in the previous chapter (pp. 120-21), Jerusalem under the Ptolemies was ruled, not by a foreign governor, but by her own priests and elders. Thus the city felt relatively tranquil and secure. Possibly during this period buildings were erected in the Tyropoeon valley between the temple area and the northwestern hill of Jerusalem. Also, the so-called tombs of Absalom and of others in the Kidron valley may date from this era.

The Seleucid rule of Jerusalem began in 198 B.C., with special privileges for the city's citizens such as exemption from taxation for three years. Soon, however, the internal factional struggles described in the previous chapter (pp. 121-25) caused continual turmoil. The temple was looted by Seleucid rulers, and finally Antiochus Epiphanes in 168 B.C. desecrated the temple, destroyed much of the city and its walls, and built within it the hated Acra citadel, possibly on the southwestern hill.

The century of freedom from foreign rule under the Hasmoneans lasted from Judas Maccabeus' rededication of the temple in December 165 B.C. to Pompey's massacre of Jews in the sacred temple area in 63 B.C. At first struggles continued between the Syrian garrison in the Acra and the Jewish city proper and its temple, during which high walls were built around the temple. Finally in 141 B.C. the Jews occupied the Acra, drove out the foreigners, and refortified the city and the temple, and an era of peace within the city followed. During the reign of John Hyrcanus (134–104 B.C.) a fortress was built north of the temple. It was probably at this time that considerable expansion of the city to the north and west took place, including the building of a palace above the Tyropoeon valley and a bridge across the valley. After years of internal strife Pompey entered the city from the north-west, filled the ravine and ditch which lay before the well-fortified temple hill, besieged the temple area for three months, and then captured the sacred area and massacred the Jews who had taken refuge there.

2. Jerusalem in New Testament Times

The first twenty-five years after Jerusalem fell to the Roman general Pompey in 63 B.C. were turbulent ones for the Holy City. After several unsuccessful attempts the walls were finally rebuilt, but the enemy Parthians subsequently plundered the city. In 37 B.C., three years after he had been proclaimed king of the Jews by the Roman Senate, Herod the Great at the head of Roman troops besieged Jerusalem from the north and at terrible cost of Jewish lives captured the city and the temple area. (He did, however, prevent his Roman soldiers from entering the temple.) Thus began his thirty-three-year reign, which was to rival that of King Solomon in its magnificent building enterprises, some of which remain visible to this day.

Herod the Great's most famous building project was his reconstruction of the temple. For this purpose he doubled the size of the great temple platform to the dimensions seen today in the Muslim Sacred Precinct. The enormous and beautifully dressed stones of the wall of Herod's huge platform can still be seen in the Wailing or Western Wall and at the southeast corner where the wall rose to at least

128 feet—the height of a twelve-story building. On the platform was built a series of terraced courts, with the ornate temple itself built essentially to the dimensions of Solomon's temple, except for the huge vestibule of the east front (described in II Chron. 3:4), with its interior overlaid with gold plate.

At the northwest corner of the temple area Herod rebuilt the fortress which he named Antonia and used as a palace, with porticoes, baths, and great paved courts, and stairways and underground passages leading to the temple area. Under the present-day Convent of the Sisters of Zion may still be seen the paved courtyard of this huge building complex, "with the wheelruts of chariots and with the 'board' of the games" played by the Roman soldiers.[6]

Part of a second fortress rebuilt by Herod and used as a new royal palace on the western hill of Jerusalem remains today in the massive foundation stones of the so-called Tower of David. In addition Herod built two viaducts across the Tyropoeon valley to connect the western hill with the temple area on the east, as well as a theater, an amphitheater, and a hippodrome. All these grandiose building operations required considerable filling in of the valleys of hilly Jerusalem and obviously resulted in considerable change from the original contours of the city.

The events connected with the city of Jerusalem in the lifetime of Jesus begin with his visit to the city at Passover time when he was twelve years old (Luke 2:41-51). This would have been in about A.D. 6, when Herod's son Archelaus was banished to Gaul to end his ten-year rule in Jerusalem.

The procurators who succeeded Archelaus preferred to rule from Caesarea, their seacoast capital, and only to live in the Herodian palace in Jerusalem on their occasional visits to the city. The best-known of these procurators, Pontius Pilate, followed the example of Herod the Great in building a second aqueduct to bring water from near Bethlehem to the city of Jerusalem.

During the rule of the procurators, notably Pontius Pilate, Jesus visited the city on several occasions, according to the Gospel of John. The healing of the lame man at the "pool, in Hebrew called Bethzatha" (John 5:1-18) may well have taken place at the traditional site north of the temple area, now under the church belonging to the White Fathers. Another probably authentic spot is the praetorium in Herod's Antonia, with the great stone pavement more than 150 feet square, where the soldiers mocked Jesus, and Pilate condemned him to death (Matt. 27:15-31; Mark 15:6-20; Luke 23:13-25; John 19:12-16).

These places are now many feet below the present ground level in the Old City of Jerusalem, and this fact reminds us that the centuries of building and rebuilding of the often embattled city of Jerusalem in the subsequent two millennia makes it improbable that, except for the Herodian masonry mentioned above, we can exactly retrace the footsteps of Jesus. Nevertheless the Via Dolorosa, which runs, with its traditional fourteen stations of the cross, from the Antonia to the present-day Church of the Holy Sepulchre, may follow essentially the path of our Lord on that last Holy Week journey.

Obviously the Palm Sunday procession down the Mount of Olives east of the city, the site also of the Ascension, may readily be envisaged as to general location. The centuries-old belief that both Calvary or Golgotha and the place of Jesus' burial were in or near the Church of the Holy Sepulchre, on the site of a church built

155

at least as early as the fourth century A.D., has been made more nearly probable by evidence that this location was outside the city wall in Jesus' day, even though the atmosphere of the present-day Garden Tomb, Gordon's Calvary, north of the Old City may feel more authentic.[7]

According to the accounts in the Acts of the Apostles, many key events in the earliest years of the Christian church took place in and around the Jerusalem temple built by Herod the Great. Subsequently Herod Agrippa I, grandson of Herod the Great, gained everlasting infamy among Christians by his harsh treatment of the apostolic church in Jerusalem; he killed James and imprisoned Peter (Acts 12:1-3). This activity may have been among the reasons for his popularity with the Jews, however, for his brief reign was a period of prosperity in which he very generously supported the temple worship, constructed a fine paved street running up the eastern side of the central valley of the city, and built a north wall approximately on the line of the present north wall of the Old City. King David's Jerusalem had been eleven acres in area. Now, a thousand years later, Herod Agrippa's city had grown to 310 acres![8]

From the death of Herod Agrippa I in A.D. 44 to the destruction of Jerusalem and its temple in A.D. 70, as we have seen in the previous chapter (pp. 136-38), there was a crescendo of internal strife in the city. One bright spot in this period was the tomb-building of a convert to Judaism, Queen Helen of Adiabene, whose impressive tomb, made for herself and family and traditionally called the Tombs of the Kings, may be seen today a short distance north of the Old City.

The sad fact is that the final devastation of Jerusalem was apparently brought about in large measure by the bloody struggles of fanatical terrorist Jewish rebels such as the Sicarii against more moderate fellow Jews as well as by the punitive forces of the Romans. In the war of 66–70 the Romans constructed a wall more than five miles long around the city to prevent its defenders from breaking out in the famine conditions of the final siege of 70. The enormous blocks of this wall may be those visible today in a wall excavated north of the present Old City.

The senseless fighting and killing among the various Jewish factions has been declared to be more horrible than the siege itself. The troops of Titus gradually penetrated the city from the northwest. According to Josephus' account the temple, the last stronghold of the Jewish rebels, finally went up in flames in August, 70, upon the rejection of an offer that he, Josephus, might serve as mediator and so save this holy place.

In the subsequent second and final Jewish revolt of 132–34 Jerusalem was briefly freed from Roman rule by Simon ben Kozeba, but was soon recaptured by the Romans. Thereupon it became a Roman colony, the Colonia Aelia Capitolina, and a shrine dedicated to Jupiter was built in the temple area. Thus, in fact, the destruction of the temple in A.D. 70 ended Judaism's control of the Holy City until our present century, almost two thousand years later.

3. Jerusalem as the Metropolis of Christendom

In the six hundred years after A.D. 70, when Jerusalem had been left in ruins by the future Roman emperor Titus, the city eventually became in effect the world center of Gentile Christianity. Hence in this period the Holy City has been appropriately called the "metropolis of Christ-endom." [9]

True, before the final siege of Jerusalem the former Christian community of the Holy City had fled across the Jordan River to Pella. But another Christian community was soon thereafter reestablished in Jerusalem, now free from the previous persecution by Judaism. And when the emperor Hadrian obliterated Jerusalem by establishing the colony of Aelia Capitolina on top of it in 135, no Jew was allowed to settle in the new Roman city; instead, a Gentile population resettled the area. Hence Gentile internal control, first of Roman religions, then later of Christen-dom, was assured.

The old city of David on the eastern ridge was now abandoned. The new city had essentially the area of the present-day Old City of Jerusalem. Its main north-south thoroughfare was a columned street extending south and slightly southwest from the present-day Damascus Gate. The old temple area was kept as an open square. Statues of the emperor Hadrian and of the god Jupiter and monu-mental gateways were erected in various parts of the city.

When the emperor Constantine made Christianity the official religion of the Roman Empire in A.D. 313, Jerusalem became the world center for all Christendom—a position which it has retained in the hearts of Christians from that day to this. In the subsequent Byzantine period Christian pilgrims from all over the world flocked to the Holy City, and many accounts of their visits survive.

The greatest monument of the Byzantine period in Jerusalem was, and is still, the Church of the Holy Sepulchre, built by Queen Helena, Constantine's mother, in about 325. One of the arguments for its authenticity as being on the site of Jesus' resurrection is that the church was deliberately built on that spot to rechristianize the site because a Roman temple with sexually licentious rites dedicated to the goddess Venus had previously been erected there intentionally to desecrate the holy tomb of our Lord.

The fifth and sixth centuries saw tremendous building of churches, monasteries, and hospices in and around Jerusalem as the city became the metropolis of Christendom. One pilgrim of the sixth century says he counted twenty-four churches on the Mount of Olives alone. The famous sixth-century mosaic map set in the floor of a church in Madeba in Transjordan depicts Jerusalem as a city fortified by a wall with twenty-one towers and six gates. Prominent on the map are the Church of the Holy Sepulchre, the Church of St. Anne the mother of Mary, and a number of other churches.

The end of Jerusalem's preeminence as the effective center of world Christendom came about with the threat to the Byzantine Empire from the rising power of the Sassanid Persians. After overrunning Syria, the Persians, aided by the Samaritans and the Jews, sacked Jerusalem in 614. According to some accounts over thirty-three thousand of Jerusalem's inhabitants were massacred, and the churches and monuments of Christendom went up in flames. Although there was a subsequent period of Byzantine reconstruction culminating in a solemn procession from the Golden Gate to the Church of the Holy Sepulchre on March 23, 630, Christendom's ascendency in the Holy City has never been recovered.

4. Jerusalem Under the Muslims

The Arabian prophet Mohammed (?570–632) regarded himself, and has always been regarded by his Muslim

159

followers, as one standing in the line of succession of Abraham, David, Solomon, and Jesus, all venerated by Muslims as prophets. Jerusalem's Arabic name is El Quds, "Holiness," and in fact until nine years before his death Mohammed directed that prayers to the one God Allah should be spoken facing Jerusalem, not Mecca or Medina, the other cities holy to Islam. Hence, it is not surprising that later Muslim tradition declared that Mohammed worshiped in company with his prophetic predecessors Abraham, Moses, and Jesus in what is now the Muslim Sacred Precinct, the Haram esh-Sherif, where Abraham had nearly sacrificed Isaac and the temple of Solomon once stood. Immediately thereafter, says tradition, Mohammed ascended from that sacred spot up a ladder of light to the presence of God in the seventh heaven.

The rapid Muslim conquest of the Near East led to a war of faiths between the Christian Byzantine Empire and Islam, and since Islam enjoined holy war, the very moderate treatment of Jerusalem by the conquering Muslims was remarkable. Technically Jerusalem fell to the Arabs when the Byzantine emperor Heraclius lost Syria and Palestine in 636. Actually it was two years later that the inhabitants of Jerusalem invited the Muslim caliph Omar to come to Jerusalem to negotiate a peace treaty. When the caliph visited the Church of the Holy Sepulchre, then called the Church of the Resurrection, and it was time for Muslim prayer, he went outside the church to pray, despite the Christian patriarch's invitation to pray inside the church. The caliph did this lest in the future Muslims should regard his praying inside as authorizing the Muslims to take over the church. For him Jerusalem was the Holy City of both faiths.

Obviously, the site of Solomon's temple was the focus

of attention for Muslim builders, as they envisaged Mohammed as successor to both Jewish and Christian faiths. Hence by 691 the Dome of the Rock, one of the most beautiful buildings in the world, was completed in the center of Herod's temple platform. To the south within the Sacred Precinct was erected the Aqsa Mosque, still the main Muslim shrine in Jerusalem. The close association of Islam with Christianity in the Muslim popular mind is shown by the tradition that in the Aqsa Mosque the prayer niche oriented toward Mecca was associated with the Annunciation to Mary and a nearby stone basin marks the location where Jesus as a boy spoke in the temple.[10] The architectural beauty of these buildings is largely due to the use of Byzantine forms. (The Dome of the Rock is a Byzantine rotunda on an octagonal base.)

On the whole, the first period of Muslim rule in Jerusalem, which lasted over 450 years, from 638 to 1099, was one of tolerance and relative peace within the city. Such persecutions as did take place there during this era were reflections of the struggles between the Byzantine and Muslim powers outside Palestine. Early in the eleventh century the Church of the Holy Sepulchre was so badly damaged that it was almost destroyed, but in 1037 it was rebuilt by special agreement between the Byzantine emperor and the caliph. Finally, when the Muslims put the city in a state of protective siege in 1099, on the eve of the First Crusade, native Christians were evacuated from Jerusalem.

For nearly a century, 1099 to 1187, Jerusalem was temporarily lost to the Muslims. The First Crusade, the first of several Christian military expeditions to recover the Holy Land from the forces of Islam, had been launched in 1096. It was motivated at least in part by the desire to

161

assert the authority of Rome over the East as the Muslim Empire was disintegrating.

At last, at sunset on June 7, 1099, after a long military trek through Asia Minor, Syria, and Palestine, the European feudal lords Godfrey of Bouillon, Robert of Flanders, Robert of Normandy, and Raymond of Toulouse and their troops encamped before the Jaffa Gate, the Damascus Gate, the Herod Gate, and the western part of the south wall of Jerusalem, respectively. Finally on July 15 the walls were stormed, and an unbelievably savage massacre of the Muslim inhabitants followed. According to one account ten thousand Muslims were beheaded in the Aqsa Mosque alone, and the paved area of the Sacred Precinct was knee-deep in corpses and blood. Such was the triumph of the Cross over the Crescent!

On Christmas Day, 1100, Godfrey of Bouillon's brother Baldwin was crowned king of the newly established Latin Kingdom of Jerusalem, and for nearly ninety years a series of Frankish kings occupied the throne. Under these rulers the Dome of the Rock and the Mosque of Omar became Christian churches, and a number of new churches were built in the city. Finally the Muslim sultan Saladin, who had reconquered Palestine in a series of battles, notably that near Tiberias in 1187, accepted the surrender of Jerusalem on October 2, 1189. Seven days later he led public worship in the now recleansed Aqsa Mosque. Thus, with little bloodshed in Jerusalem, the Crescent triumphed over the Cross once again—and many native Christians rejoiced in the return of Muslim toleration.

Only twice more before the end of the Crusades in 1272 was there a European Christian challenge to Muslim control of Jerusalem. The first lasted for several agonizing days in 1192 when, during the Third Crusade, Richard I of

England besieged the city but withdrew without taking it. The second took place following the Sixth Crusade, and was a fifteen-year period from 1229 to 1244 when by treaty the German emperor Frederick II, sympathetic to Islam because he had spent most of his life in half-Arab Sicily, was the titular king of Jerusalem. Finally in 1244 a band of Turks took the city and burned the Church of the Holy Sepulchre. Thus Jerusalem passed finally out of the hands of the Christian West.

The final seven hundred years of Muslim control of Jerusalem—from the end of the Crusades to the close of the First World War—were an era readily divisible into two periods of at least nominal external foreign control, first from the south, then from the north. The control from the south was that of the dynasties of Mamluk sultans of Egypt who ruled the Muslim territories from 1261 to 1520. In these nearly three centuries little of note seems to have happened in Jerusalem except for certain rebuilding of walls and of Herod the Great's palace by the Jaffa Gate.

By the middle of the fifteenth century, however, a new era was beginning. The fall of Constantinople to the Ottoman Turks in 1453 marks a watershed in Western history. Early in the following century the struggle for Palestine between the Ottoman Turks in the north and the Egyptian Mamluk sultans in the south came to a head (this was not unlike the earlier struggles between Assyria and Egypt or between the Seleucids and the Ptolemies). With the Turkish victory over the Mamluks in 1517, a period of Turkish rule lasting exactly four centuries began in Palestine.

This Ottoman Turkish rule was marked first by the rebuilding of the walls of the city by the sultan Suleiman the Magnificent in 1538–41. Herodian blocks of stone and whole sections of Byzantine and Mamluk work such as St. Stephen's Gate were used. The Golden Gate in the east wall of the Muslim Sacred Precinct was walled up because of the tradition that the Jewish-Christian Messiah would some day enter the city through that gate. His entrance must be made difficult, to say the least! A good example of Suleiman's work is the present-day Damascus Gate. Actually we owe much of the appearance of today's Old City of Jerusalem to this great Muslim builder.

For most of these centuries of Turkish rule Jerusalem was little noticed politically. It was but a small semi-independent district, at times under the control of a provincial Turkish governor-general in Beirut. During these years their religion, Islam, was the only common bond between the Turks and the Arabs they ruled, including those in Palestine. There was no common bond of race, or of language except for the Arabic of the Koran. The military overlords, the Turks, came to despise the Arabs, who in turn were proud of their Arabian history and heritage. Hence there grew up movements of revolt among the Arabs which were put down by the Turks with an iron hand.

The last half of the nineteenth century brought new facets to the already complicated cultural forces in Jerusalem and Palestine. Spurred on by the intellectual ferment in Europe and by the opening of the Middle East to Western travel and Christian missions, a minority of younger Arabs began to demand educational, economic, and national independence from their Turkish overlords. There was even unheard-of cooperation between Muslim and Christian Arabs in a renaissance of Arab culture. The first European consulate, that of Great Britain, had been established in Jerusalem in 1839, and in 1841 was

164

originated the Anglican bishopric of Jerusalem, now the Cathedral Church of St. George, the seat of an archbishop of the Church of England. As the century drew to a close the fires of Arab nationalism were burning brightly—for example, in certain Arab families of Jerusalem who were struggling for independence from Turkish domination.

Alongside this rising tide of Arab nationalism in Jerusalem and Palestine at the end of the nineteenth century must be placed another very significant movement: the founding and growth of Jewish Zionism. Large numbers of Jews, refugees from persecution in Europe and elsewhere, as well as pious Jews who obtained their lifelong desire of ending their days in such sacred spots as Jerusalem, had settled in the Holy Land. Sir Moses Montefiore, a Jewish banker in London, estimated the Jewish population of all Palestine in 1837 to be eight thousand.

The founder of the movement called Zionism is generally considered to be Theodor Herzl, a Hungarian Jew who, incensed by the social and economic ostracism of Jews in the cities of Western Europe, presided over the First Zionist Congress held at Basel, Switzerland, in 1897. The stated objective of the movement included the colonization of Palestine by Jewish agricultural and industrial workers. In a few years, after some sharp differences of opinion within the Zionist movement as to whether the new Jewish National Home must be in Palestine or could be in some other part of the world, such as Uganda or South America, the Zionist movement determined that Palestine must be the Jewish National Home.

The clash of the two nationalisms, Arab and Jewish, which has taken place in the twentieth century, would seem to have been unavoidable. And, of course, the holy city of Jerusalem has inevitably been at the center of the struggle, although the city's destiny has been fashioned, as frequently in its centuries of history, not primarily by its own internal struggles, but by great foreign powers outside.

With the conclusion of World War I in 1918, the Ottoman Empire was divided among the victorious Western Allies, and Britain was soon to have administrative control of Jerusalem and Palestine. Thus ended more than twelve hundred years of Muslim domination of Jerusalem. Once again the city was the victim of a struggle between foreign powers.

How often in three thousand years the city of Jerusalem has been cruelly treated by mighty foreign invaders: devastated by the Babylonians in 586 B.C., by the Romans in A.D. 70, by the Persians in A.D. 614—and many other times severely damaged. But the Holy City has always been rebuilt and has risen again phoenixlike out of the ashes! And how many different allegiances, loyalties— and rulers and even changing inhabitants—these three millennia have brought to this world-famous city: the city of David and his people the Jews for the eleven hundred years of biblical times; the capital of Christendom for six hundred years and for an additional century during the Crusades; and a Muslim holy city for twelve hundred years until the beginning of the present century!

Surely these three faiths—Judaism, Christianity, Islam—have a never-to-be-forgotten historical and spiritual investment in this unique city of the Holy Land. In 1976 the question may be asked: Will history once again be repeated? Will the destiny of the Holy City once more be determined, not by its own citizens, divided though they be, but by superpowers—nations and national alliances—settling their international disputes for their own ends?

Notes

1. Three of the best summaries of the history of Jerusalem, upon which this present writer has drawn heavily, are: Millar Burrows, "Jerusalem," *Interpreter's Dictionary of the Bible*, vol. 2, pp. 843-66; John Gray, *A History of Jerusalem* (London: Robert Hale, 1969); and Kathleen M. Kenyon, *Jerusalem: Excavating 3000 Years of History* (New York: McGraw Hill Book Co., 1968).
2. So dated by Kenyon, *Jerusalem*, p. 19.
3. Millar Burrows interprets the Israelites' action simply as fighting their way to the opening of the shaft and so cutting off the Jebusites' water supply ("Jerusalem," p. 848).
4. After David's bringing of the ark to Jerusalem and Solomon's building of the temple the term *Zion* comes to have a primarily religious connotation. Originally it apparently referred to the temple hill and the area of "the city of David" to the south of the temple. In much later tradition the reference was to the southwestern hill of the city where eventually a Christian basilica was built, supposedly on the site of the upper room of the Lord's Supper and Pentecost. However, *Zion* came to mean all Jerusalem as religious capital. In both Jewish and Christian parlance the term came to be used to refer to "the Holy City," whether earthly Jerusalem or the heavenly city to which all the devout wish to be "marching." Strictly speaking, "Zionism" is a movement which originated in the late 1800s, having as its goal the resettlement of Jews in Palestine, and which now seeks to help Israel as a national Jewish state.
5. Probably the great high altar of sacrifice to the east of the temple, not the temple itself, stood over the large rock which is under the present Muslim Dome of the Rock.
6. Gray, *History of Jerusalem*, p. 158.
7. For a more detailed account of the sites in Jerusalem

associated with the lifetime of Jesus consult Burrows. "Jerusalem," pp. 860-63.

8. So Kenyon, *Jerusalem*, p. 155. For a brief popular account of recent excavations of the area around the Herodian temple platform see Christopher L. Hallowell. "The Glory That Was Jerusalem," *Natural History* (New York: American Museum of Natural History), 82. no. 10 (December, 1973). pp. 38-49. The best and most complete account of recent excavations in Jerusalem is the excellent 136-page illustrated volume *Jerusalem Revealed: Archaeology in the Holy City 1968–1974* (Jerusalem: The Israel Exploration Society, 1975).

9. Gray, *History of Jerusalem*, pp. 194-209.

10. *Ibid.*, p. 222.

10

The Past
Within the Present

We have now seen the roots—geographical, economic, political, cultural, religious—of the present Middle East conflict. With this background it is the aim of this chapter to give a factual account of the chief events of the twentieth century. This is done in the hopes that the reader will gain an informed understanding on which to make judgments concerning the rights and wrongs of, and possible solutions to, this vastly complex situation.

1. Nationalisms and the End of Turkish Rule

The first two decades of the twentieth century witnessed the rapid growth of two nationalisms in the Middle East and the collapse of the Ottoman Empire which had ruled the area for four centuries.

Arab nationalism, the rise of which was described briefly in the last chapter (pp. 164-65), increased in intensity as the Arabs sought to throw off the yoke of their Turkish rulers, and several outstanding Arab families led their fellow Arabs in moves for independence. One of these was the Hashemite family, which claimed noble descent from the clan of the prophet Mohammed. (The official name of present-day Jordan is the Hashemite Kingdom of Jordan, and its king, Hussein, is the great-grandson of Sherif Hussein of Mecca in Saudi

Arabia, who led a revolt against the Ottoman Turks.) During the First World War, to encourage the Arabs to rebel against the Turks, who were Germany's allies, Sir Henry McMahon, the British high commissioner in Egypt, in 1915–16 entered into a gentleman's agreement with them that upon the expulsion of the Turks, the Arab lands (except for certain non-Arab areas in Syria) should be independent, from the Anatolian foothills to the Indian Ocean, and from the Persian border to the Mediterranean. What was unknown to the Arabs, until it was revealed by the Russians in December, 1917, was that by the Sykes-Picot Agreement of May, 1916, the British and French were planning to divide up the Ottoman Empire—Syria and Lebanon to go to France, and Palestine and Iraq to Britain.

These two agreements made by Western powers, irreconcilable as they were, were to come into conflict with yet a third, the famous Balfour Declaration dated November 2, 1917. This was a letter from Arthur James Balfour, then foreign secretary in the British coalition war cabinet of David Lloyd George, to Baron Walter Rothschild, a prominent British Jewish Zionist. The letter reads as follows:

Dear Lord Rothschild,

I have much pleasure in conveying to you, on behalf of His Majesty's Government, the following declaration of sympathy with Jewish Zionist aspirations which has been submitted to, and approved by, the Cabinet.

"His Majesty's Government view with favour the establishment in Palestine of a National Home for the Jewish people, and will use their best endeavours to facilitate the achievement of this object, it being clearly understood that nothing shall be done which may prejudice the civil and religious rights of existing non-Jewish communities in

Palestine, or the rights and political status enjoyed by Jews in any other country."

I should be grateful if you would bring this declaration to the knowledge of the Zionist Federation.

(signed)
Arthur James Balfour[1]

This declaration, which was released and published immediately, gave strong impetus to the competing nationalism, Jewish Zionism. From the origins of modern Zionism, which were briefly described in the last chapter (pp. 165-66), a number of Jews, many of them refugees from Russia, had settled in the Holy Land. By 1914 there were 85,000 Jews in Palestine out of a total population of 739,000.[2]

The Balfour Declaration had largely come about through the persevering, single-minded devotion of the hard-driving leader of Zionism in the first half of this century, Chaim Weizmann, a Russian-born scientist whose chemical discoveries aided Britain's war effort and who was later to become the first president of the state of Israel from 1949 until his death in 1952. Actually, however, the Balfour Declaration was disappointingly less vigorous than Weizmann and some British Jews would have liked. Rather than simply build a Jewish National Home *in* Palestine, they preferred making Palestine *the* Jewish National Home.

In this period there was strong opposition among Jews to the practical Zionism which came primarily from Eastern European Jews. Even within Zionist circles some, especially in Britain and Western Europe, preferred only a theoretical Zionism which was concerned with a Jewish home simply as a relief measure for the oppressed Jews of the world. In fact, just as many Arabs have little or no nationalistic aspirations or interest, so opposition to

171

Zionism among Jews persists to this day. This opposition may have widely differing motivations. On the one hand, there is the extreme anti-Zionism of certain pious ultra-orthodox Hasidic Jews, such as those who do not support the present state of Israel, because they regard it as a predominantly secular state—ancient Israel, they say, cannot be restored by any human hand, only by the Messiah when he comes! [3] At the opposite extreme are the quite secularized Jews who desire as complete an assimilation as possible into the culture of the Western nation in which they live. Perhaps a middle ground between these extremes includes those Jews who oppose Zionism because they prefer that non-Jews see Jews as a religious denomination rather than a national group.

Many Jews are Zionists, however, because they see the establishment of a national Jewish state in Palestine, regardless of how secular the state may be, not only as the fulfillment of the dream of ancient Israel, but also as a very important part of the complete expression of what it means religiously and culturally to be a Jew. For them Judaism without a Jewish national state in the Holy Land would be a somewhat emasculated Judaism. The ultimate success of Zionism in establishing the present state of Israel was due in no small part to Weizmann's persistence in uniting practical and theoretical Zionism and overcoming anti-Zionist opposition among Jews, as well as selling his ideas to counsels of state.

While these political operations—the McMahon Correspondence, the Sykes-Picot Agreement, and the Balfour Declaration—were going on in diplomatic circles, World War I was being bitterly fought on the battlefield. In the Middle East, Egypt was occupied and the Sinai traversed by the British army, and moving northward into Palestine,

on November 7, 1917, just five days after the promulga-
tion of the Balfour Declaration, General Sir Edmund
Allenby won a decisive battle against the Turkish forces at
Gaza. On December 9, 1917, after more hard-fought
battles, General Allenby reverently entered Jerusalem on
foot by the Jaffa Gate and had the following proclamation
read to the people in English, French, Italian, Arabic, and
Hebrew:

To the inhabitants of Jerusalem the Blessed and the people
dwelling in the vicinity. The defeat inflicted upon the Turks by
the troops under my command has resulted in the occupation of
your city by my forces. I therefore here and now proclaim it to be
under martial law, under which form of administration it will
remain so long as military considerations make it necessary.
However, lest any of you be alarmed because of your experience
at the hands of the enemy who has retired, I hereby inform you
that it is my desire that every person should pursue his lawful
business without fear of interruption.

Furthermore, since your city is regarded with affection by the
adherents of three of the great religions of mankind, and its soil
has been consecrated by the prayers and pilgrimages of
multitudes of devout people of these three religions for many
centuries, therefore, do I make known to you that every sacred
building, monument, holy spot, traditional shrine, endowment,
pious bequest, or customary place of prayer, of whatsoever form
of the three religions, will be maintained and protected
according to the existing customs and beliefs of those to whose
faiths they are sacred.[4]

Nine months later, on September 18, 1918, Allenby's
victory at Megiddo, that ancient battleground, at last gave
the British control of Syria and Palestine.

Victory over the Turks was due to the skillful combin-
ing of Allenby's attacks with the guerrilla warfare of the
Arabs led by one of the most colorful personalities of the
First World War, Colonel T. E. Lawrence, Lawrence of

Arabia. This military and diplomatic genius had organized Arab revolt against Turkish forces; harassed the Turkish army, especially in the Transjordan area; and finally was a major contributor to the total defeat of the Turks in the Middle East and the entry of the Arabs into Damascus, the capital of Syria.

The end of Turkish domination in the Middle East thus took place shortly before the armistice which ended the First World War on November 11, 1918. But the cessation of armed conflict left severely conflicting interests to be settled in the postwar political arrangements. The Arab nationalists wanted immediate Arab independence. The Jewish Zionists wanted to build a Jewish National Home in Palestine. The British and the French wanted strategic positions in the Middle East for their own imperialist interests. Thus again appeared the very problems which beset the Middle East today—competing Arab and Jewish nationalisms and the rivalry of external big powers—problems not altogether unlike the struggles which beset this area when in biblical times ancient Israel, Judah, Syria, and Moab fought among themselves while Assyria and Egypt watched greedily from afar.

2. Life Under the British Mandate

The year 1920 was recorded by the Arabs of the Middle East as "the year of catastrophe." This was the year when, instead of the promised independence from external control, the French occupied Damascus and it became obvious that Palestine, then on both sides of the Jordan River, would shortly become a mandated territory under British rule. And so Palestine was to remain for twenty-eight years.

Although the British mandate over Palestine was not put into effect until 1922, this political arrangement in the Middle East was the outcome of the Versailles Peace Conference at the end of World War I. At that conference Lawrence of Arabia, who was the Arabs' hero, the "uncrowned King of Arabia," had unsuccessfully pleaded for Arab independence. In 1921 he became advisor on Arab affairs to the British Colonial Office, but he was so deeply disappointed by its treatment of the Arabs and so chagrined that he had repeatedly been made to appear a traitor to his Arab friends that the next year he resigned his office, dropping out of public life and thereafter going under an assumed name.

The British had had to choose between their impossibly conflicting promises to the Jews and the Arabs. And they chose what was, and is still, regarded by the Arabs and by many observers as the typical Western imperialist colonialism of the day (though that eighteenth-century method of dealing with peoples in Asia and Africa was rapidly coming to an end). An aggressive Zionist program was underway to promote the settlement of thousands of Jews in Palestine, then to drain swamps, build up cities, and establish westernized culture. This was done on the common, but faulty, Western assumption that Palestine was backward and relatively uninhabited, a land without a people, and that such people as were there, especially after the long Turkish domination, had no effective leadership and were mostly uncultured Bedouins who felt little or no attachment to the land and were readily movable to the vast Arab lands surrounding little Palestine.[5]

It must be pointed out that in organizing and carrying out their mandate the British attempted to meet the conflicting Arab and Jewish claims. Transjordan was separated from Palestine with the provision that no Jewish colonization could take place there. In Palestine proper the British proposed the establishment of a Jewish agency and an Arab agency to act as advisory councils to the government.

Even though often critical of mandate policies and actions, the Jewish Agency moved forward rapidly with the aid of a Zionist commission in Palestine, which had been organized in July, 1918. The Arabs, however, angered by the betrayal of the promises of independence that had been made to them, refused to recognize or cooperate with the British mandate and so refused to establish the requested Arab Agency—an action somewhat comparable to their refusal after 1948 to recognize officially the existence of the state of Israel. Muslim-Christian associations through an Arab congress in 1920 had demanded an Arab government in Palestine and in 1921 had presented their case directly to London. Arab uprisings against occupying Allied forces throughout the Near East had continued from 1920 on, with riots in Jaffa in 1921 and later sporadic attacks on Jewish colonies.

Though Zionism had little effect in the Old City of Jerusalem, divided as it was into Muslim, Christian, Armenian, and Jewish quarters, a great new Jewish quarter developed northwest and west of the Old City. This area eventually became the large new section presently called West Jerusalem. A progressive institution founded by Zionism in Palestine was the now highly regarded Hebrew University, whose foundation stone was laid on Mount Scopus in July, 1918, and whose doors were opened on April 1, 1925.

As the years went by, Jewish immigration into Palestine

176

increased markedly. Between 1919 and 1923 only 35,000 Jews had entered Palestine.[6] But as a result of vigorous Zionist encouragement, on the one hand, and Nazi persecution in Germany, on the other, over 30,000 Jews entered Palestine in 1933, over 40,000 in 1934, over 60,000 in 1935, and over 29,000 in 1936.[7] Hence by 1939 Palestine was 28 percent Jewish—429,605 out of an estimated population of 1,500,000.[8]

This tremendous increase in Jewish immigration involved many sales of formerly Arab land to the new Jewish settlers, which led many Arabs to believe that Palestine would eventually become a Jewish state and that they would never achieve Arab national independence. Palestinian Arabs also felt very much discriminated against by the great powers, for by the 1930s and 1940s the surrounding Arab territories—Iraq, Egypt, Transjordan, Syria, and Lebanon—were achieving independence as separate states. Palestine was still under foreign control, and slowly but surely the Arab homeland was being usurped by foreigners.

Finally Arab resistance broke into outright rebellion which lasted from 1936 to 1939. This revolt of the Arabs was given especial impetus by a report of the British government's Palestine Royal Commission, the "Peel Report" of July, 1937, which recommended the partition of Palestine into separate Jewish and Arab states. Already the two peoples were rapidly developing two separate and distinct national communities in Palestine with separate educational, political, and economic systems. The Jewish community was approaching one-third of the population, but much better organized and stronger than the larger but divided Arab community. There was increasing Arab resentment at the sale of Arab lands, especially by absentee Arab landlords, to the immigrant Jews, which plunged evicted Arab peasants and laboring classes into a struggle for mere survival. Thus began the Palestine refugee problem which is central to the Middle East conflict today. In the years 1937 to 1939 Arabs resorted to violence—strikes, sabotage, terrorism—against the British administration of Palestine.

During this British mandate period the Jewish Zionists were also very much dissatisfied with the British administration. They felt that Britain constantly gave way to Arab violence and was dragging its feet on the Balfour Declaration of a Jewish National Home. While they reluctantly agreed to consider the partition proposal of 1937, extreme Zionists too engaged in guerrilla warfare until finally the rebellion was ended in 1939.

Well aware of the problem that unrestricted Jewish immigration and land purchases caused in Palestine, and having failed in their 1937 proposal for the partition of Palestine, the British government in May, 1939, issued a policy white paper proposing a five-year policy (to 1944) whereby Jewish immigration to Palestine would be limited. The limit would be a total of 75,000 immigrants for the five years, when the Jews would constitute one-third of the population, and after 1944 further Jewish immigration would be subject to the consent of the Arab majority. This proposal was a bitter blow to many Jewish Zionists, who had envisioned gradual development through vigorous hard work to the point where Jews would outnumber Arabs and so have clear control of the state. While Arabs were apparently favored by the British white paper, there was strong Arab resistance because of the continued Arab demand for immediate and total abolition of the mandate in order to permit Palestine to be a single independent and primarily Arab state.

The Second World War intervened, but this 1939 white paper was to provide grounds for fierce Jewish Zionist resistance to the mandate in its final period of existence, 1945–48. During the war Jews in Palestine readily cooperated with the Western allies, and by 1942 some nine thousand Palestinian Arabs also had volunteered for the British armed forces, some of them seeing active service in Greece and Italy.[9] But for Palestine the tremendous fact of the war was the holocaust, Hitler's merciless massacre of six million Jews, and the mass exodus of Jewish refugees, especially immediately after the war, many of them to Palestine and elsewhere in the Middle East.

This unspeakable horror, the holocaust, served during the war years and since to galvanize Jewish Zionism into intense activity—the Jewish National Home in Palestine must come into existence as a haven of refuge for fellow Jews!—and has to this day made a dispassionate hearing of the respective Arab and Jewish claims in the Middle East almost impossible.[10] Most notable was the intensification of Zionism in North America, both the United States and Canada. The charter of large-scale American Jewish involvement was perhaps the program enunciated on May 11, 1942, by a very important conference of the American Emergency Committee for Zionist Affairs held at the Biltmore Hotel in New York. It reads in part:

1. American Zionists assembled in this Extraordinary Conference reaffirm their unequivocal devotion to the cause of democratic freedom and international justice. . . .
2. This Conference offers a message of hope and encouragement to their fellow Jews in the Ghettos and concentration camps of

Hitler-dominated Europe and prays that their hour of liberation may not be far distant. . . .

4. In our generation, and in particular in the course of the past twenty years, the Jewish people have awakened and transformed their ancient homeland; from 50,000 at the end of the last war their numbers have increased to more than 500,000. They have made the waste places to bear fruit and the desert to blossom. Their pioneering achievements in agriculture and in industry, embodying new patterns of cooperative endeavour, have written a notable page in the history of colonization.

5. In the new values thus created, their Arab neighbours in Palestine have shared. The Jewish people in its own work of national redemption welcomes the economic, agricultural and national development of the Arab peoples and states. . . .

6. The Conference calls for the fulfillment of the original purpose of the Balfour Declaration and the Mandate. . . .

The Conference affirms its unalterable rejection of the White Paper of May 1939 and denies its moral or legal validity. . . .

8. The Conference declares that the new world order that will follow victory cannot be established on foundations of peace, justice and equality, unless the problem of Jewish homelessness is finally solved.

The Conference urges that the gates of Palestine be opened; that the Jewish agency be vested with control of immigration into Palestine and with the necessary authority for upbuilding the country, including the development of its unoccupied and uncultivated lands; and that Palestine be established as a Jewish Commonwealth integrated in the structure of the new democratic world.

Then and only then will the age-old wrong to the Jewish people be righted.[11]

Thus, with the pressure of anti-Semitic atrocities in Nazi-dominated Europe, Jewish opinion in the United States was largely won over to Zionism and to the establishment of an independent Jewish state in Palestine—hence the prevailing American Jewish sentiment for the state of Israel to this day. Public opinion in the United States was similarly won over to the Zionist views, especially because of the lack in this country of Arab spokesmen comparable to the four million American Jews with their political expertise and their influence on the mass media. Pro-Zionist resolutions were passed in thirty-three state legislatures, by the AFL-CIO, in both houses of Congress, and at the Democratic and Republican conventions in the presidential campaign of 1944.[12]

In order to deal with the problem of the flood of European Jewish refugees in the immediate postwar years, an Anglo-American commission of inquiry in 1946 suggested the immediate admission into Palestine of 100,000 such refugees and the relaxation of restrictions on land sales. In response to such suggestions Palestinian Arabs have constantly reiterated their understanding of the plight of European Jews, but they have asked why they should be made to suffer the loss of their homeland and livelihood for the sins of modern Europe!

In the last years of the mandate, 1945–48, Britain was faced with an impossible task: dealing with the growing hostility between the disparate Arab and Jewish communities and their mutual hatred of the British rule. Most difficult was the frequent illegal arrival of "coffin ships" crammed with Jewish refugees from the Nazi gas chambers. The British authorities were also plagued by the fact that extremist Jewish underground groups, especially the Irgun Zwai Leumi (National Military Organization) and the Stern Gang, resorted to violent tactics—bombings, murder, arson—against both Arabs and the British government. And Arab extremist groups retaliated in kind. Both were determined to bring the British mandate to an inglorious end. And finally, after referring the whole question of Palestine to the United Nations in February,

181

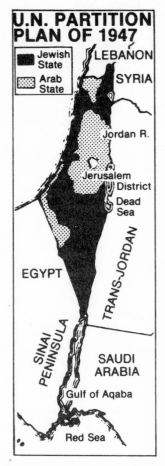

U.N. PARTITION
PLAN OF 1947
Jewish State
Arab State
LEBANON
SYRIA
Jordan R.
Jerusalem
District
Dead Sea
EGYPT
TRANS-JORDAN
SINAI PENINSULA
SAUDI ARABIA
Gulf of Aqaba
Red Sea

1947, Britain announced the following December that she would give up the mandate of Palestine on May 15, 1948.

Those last months of the British mandate, from November, 1947, to May 15, 1948, became a period of chaotic undeclared war within Palestine. Both Jewish terrorist groups, the Irgun and the Stern Gang, carried on raids against Arab villages, and even the regular army, the Haganah, joined in the fray. The Arabs too engaged in terrorism, and men and arms from five neighboring Arab states were massed on the borders of Palestine. The climax came with the massacre by Jewish extremists of 254 men, women, and children in the Arab village of Deir Yassin, on April 9, 1948, followed three days later by an Arab attack killing 77 Jewish doctors, nurses, university teachers, and students in a Red Cross convoy near Jerusalem.

With such wholesale disruption, masses of Arabs, terrified of impending destruction, fled their homes to go east to Transjordan or north to Syria or Lebanon, or even south toward Egypt. Their flight was encouraged by both

Jewish terrorists and Arab leaders, the latter promising that they would be able to return soon. Thus the British mandate ended with the division of many of Palestine's inhabitants into hostile armed camps and a mass exodus of many others.

3. The State of Israel and Four Arab-Israeli Wars

The declaration of independence of the new state of Israel was proclaimed in the city of Tel Aviv on Sabbath

ISRAEL AFTER
1948-49 WAR

LEBANON
SYRIA

Sea of Galilee

Haifa

Mediterranean Sea

Tel Aviv

Jordan R.

Jerusalem

Gaza

Port Said

Dead Sea

Suez Canal

EGYPT

JORDAN

Gulf of Suez

eve, May 14, 1948, and British control of Palestine ended officially that night. The creation and establishment of the new country had been authorized by a United Nations General Assembly resolution[13] passed on November 29, 1947, by a vote of thirty-three to thirteen with ten abstentions and one absentee. This resolution provided that "independent Arab and Jewish States and the Special International Regime for the City of Jerusalem, set forth in part III of this plan, shall come into existence in Palestine two months after the evacuation of the armed forces of the mandatory Power has been completed but in any case not later than 1 October 1948."

The Jews had accepted the partition plan proposed by the United Nations with its provision for a Jewish state, but the Arabs of Palestine were violently opposed to the dismemberment of what they considered to be their homeland. Much of the fighting between Arabs and Jews from November, 1947, to May, 1948, when Israel came into existence, was an attempt by both sides to capture as much territory as possible.

On May 15, 1948, the day after the new Jewish state of Israel was launched, the first Arab-Israeli war began in earnest. At once the so-called Palestinian Arab Liberation Army and troops coming in from Egypt, Iraq, Syria, and Transjordan (but not Lebanon) attacked Israel's outnumbered forces. At first it seemed as though little Israel would soon suffer defeat, but by the end of December the disunited Arab forces had been virtually routed. A cease-fire was finally arranged in July, 1949, by Ralph Bunche of the U.N. Secretariat, successor to Count Folke Bernadotte of Sweden, who had been killed in Jerusalem by Jewish terrorists. About 700,000 Arabs fled or were driven from their homes and became refugees in the Arab countries around Israel.

Cease-fire agreements did not establish boundaries for the new state of Israel, only the stipulation that neither side would advance beyond the armistice line. The result was a crazy, zigzag boundary line running from north to south, sometimes even separating a village from its well or its accustomed farmland. But Israel ended up with not only all the territory the U.N. proposal had originally provided for but also about half of the land which had been planned for the Arab state. In fact, the new state of Israel held all of Palestine except the territory known as the West Bank of the Jordan, the Old City of Jerusalem, and the Gaza Strip. The West Bank and the Old City of Jerusalem were to be under the control of the Hashemite Kingdom of Jordan, with its capital Amman (ancient Rabbath-Ammon), and the Gaza Strip on the southwest was to be administered by Egypt. A U.N. truce supervision organization was established to investigate any reports of new fighting between Arabs and Israelis.

For almost the next two decades the Holy City was a divided city with a wall and a no-man's-land of barbed wire and minefields between the Old City, held by the Arabs on the east, and the newer, Jewish sector on the west. West Jerusalem became the capital of Israel, but it was not recognized as such by most countries having diplomatic relations with Israel, because of the U.N. plan to make Jerusalem an international city.

The Jews were outraged that Jews were banned from the Old City, that the Jewish Quarter in the Old City had been demolished and Jewish cemeteries desecrated, and, perhaps most of all, that no Jew could make his way eastward through the Mandelbaum Gate to worship at the

185

holy Wailing Wall as his ancestors had done for centuries. And displaced Arabs were outraged as they looked toward the west over the wall and either literally or in imagination saw their former homes, where once they had had friendly relations with Jewish neighbors, now occupied by others, without the hope of the slightest remuneration. Only once a year at Christmastime could even Christians cross through the Mandelbaum Gate for a brief family reunion.

The phenomenal development of the new state of Israel—economically, politically, industrially, agriculturally, and in many other ways—was originally due in no small measure to the indefatigable vigor and leadership of the new state's first prime minister, David Ben-Gurion. This devoted Zionist leader served as prime minister and minister of defense almost continuously from 1948 until 1963. With the help through the years of tremendous financial aid from American Jews, the economy of Israel, despite vast military expenditures and in spite of poor natural resources, has grown at the rate of about 10 percent annually. The first Israeli census, taken in 1948, gave the population of Israel as 872,678; the second census, in 1961, as 2,194,249. Arabs who remained in Israel constitute about 10 percent of the population.[14]

It was Ben-Gurion's policy for this Jewish state that no Arab who fled the country should ever be permitted to return. Many of the Arabs living in Israel have prospered economically, and they have political rights such as representation in the parliament, the Knesset. However, limited as they are by restrictions on travel from their homes and other measures regarded as oppressive, and under continual surveillance because of the threats and terrorism from the surrounding Arab world, the Arabs in

Israel chafe under their minority status as second-class citizens in a Jewish state comprised of 90 percent Jews.

It is estimated that there are some 14,000,000 Jews living in the world today, of whom over 5,700,000 are in the United States, 2,500,000 in Russia, and 2,300,000 in Israel.[15] Some 1,250,000 Jews have immigrated into Israel from all parts of the world. The majority of these immigrants used to come from Europe. Most were Ashkenazim, from Germany, Poland, and Russia. Some were Sephardim, from Spanish and Portuguese families. But in recent years half or more of the immigrant Jews are Oriental—dark-skinned Jews from Asian and African countries, including Jewish refugees from Arab countries. Thus in present-day Israel, since Israel is very westernized and both government and industry are controlled primarily by the European Jews, there is considerable dissatisfaction among the Oriental Jews and, therefore, tension between the two groups. The growing number of young Jews born in Israel, called sabras, take real pride in their country and may prefer to be considered more Israeli[16] than Jewish.

With this diversity and growing density of Jewish population in the small state of Israel, it is understandable that there are widely divergent views on perhaps every subject, including the treatment of Arabs. But the barrage of threats from the outside Arab world in times of crisis has welded Israel's people into a strong fighting force, as has been seen in the several Arab-Israeli wars.

On May 15, 1948, the day after Israel was proclaimed an independent state, the governments of the Arab League— then composed of seven states, Iraq, Saudi Arabia, Lebanon, Yemen, Transjordan, Egypt, and Syria—issued a statement defending their invasion of the new Jewish state.[17] After describing the history of the West's broken promises to the Arab world and declaring Palestine to be an Arab country, and stating that henceforth under the charter of the United Nations Palestine should revert to its inhabitants, they declared that

the only just solution of the Palestine problem is the establishment of a unitary Palestinian State, whereby its inhabitants will enjoy complete equality before the law, (and whereby) minorities will be assured of all the guarantees recognized in democratic constitutional countries, and (whereby) the holy places will be preserved and the right of access thereto guaranteed.

On this basis the Arab countries surrounding Israel have to this day refused even to recognize officially Israel's existence as a state. In addition nearly a million Arab refugees in Gaza, Jordan, Syria, Lebanon, and Egypt have cried out for revenge and a chance "to go home." Hence there have been frequent Palestinian terrorist attacks in Israel, not altogether unlike the tactics used earlier by the Jewish terrorist gangs against the British to force the end of the British mandate. The chief Arab demand continues to be for a unified independent Palestinian state in which once more, as before 1918, Arab and Jew can live peacefully side by side. But how could the clock of history possibly thus be turned back?

The second Arab-Israeli war, the conflict of 1956, was only partially precipitated by these continuing problems of Palestinian refugees and Arab independence movements. The war was also fought over freedom of navigation in the Gulf of Aqaba and the Suez Canal. Partly in revenge for Israel's refusal to permit Palestinian refugees to return, Israeli ships were blockaded in the canal and in the gulf, where Israel was developing a port at Elath.

After provocation from Arab terrorist raids from Egypt through the Gaza Strip, Israel attacked the Gaza Strip in February, 1955. Thirty-eight Egyptian soldiers were killed, and thirty-one wounded. Rebuffed by the refusal of the Western nations to supply arms and of the United States to help build the Aswan High Dam, President Gamal Abdel Nasser of Egypt turned to Russia for help, and in July, 1956, he nationalized the Suez Canal and so eliminated its British and French management.

With the support of Great Britain and France, Israel saw a chance to settle the score with Egypt. On October 29, 1956, Israeli tanks invaded Sinai, supported by French planes. By November 5 the Israelis occupied the Gaza Strip and the Sinai Peninsula to its southern tip at Sharm el Sheikh, and the British and French tried to retake the Suez Canal by force and did succeed in controlling the northern entrance to the canal.

To restore peace the United States and Russia, together with the United Nations, persuaded Britain and France to withdraw. A cease-fire which had been demanded by the U.N. General Assembly in emergency session was achieved on November 6, and on November 15 a U.N. emergency force arrived in Egypt to keep the peace. This force was stationed in Egypt along the Israeli border. Israel has consistently refused to permit U.N. troops on its land. Finally in March, 1957, Israel withdrew its forces to the original 1949 cease-fire lines with the warning that "interference, by armed force, with ships of Israel flag exercising free and innocent passage in the Gulf of Aqaba and through the Straits of Tiran, will be regarded by Israel as an attack entitling it to exercise its inherent right of self-defence under Article 51 of the United Nations Charter and to take all such measures as are necessary to

189

ensure the free and innocent passage of its ships in the Gulf and in the Straits."[18]

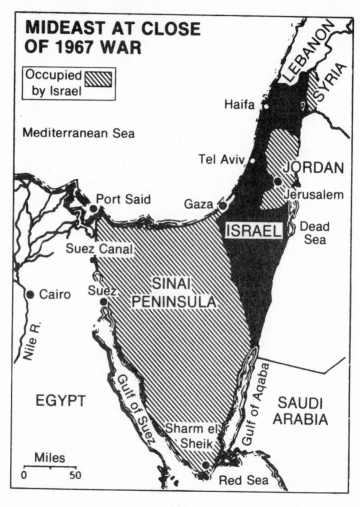

By all odds the most important for the future of the Middle East was the third Arab-Israeli war, which took place on six memorable days ten years later, June 5–10, 1967. This Six-Day War was preceded by growing dissension among the Arab countries, especially between the conservative, oil-rich Arab kingdoms and sheikdoms such as Saudi Arabia and Kuwait, on the one hand, and the revolutionary regimes in Egypt, Syria, Iraq, and Algeria, on the other. Despite this typical Arab disunity, however, both sides agreed on one thing—their antagonism toward Israel. Gradually President Nasser of Egypt became the presumed spokesman for the Arab world.

During the period between the 1956 and 1967 wars the Arab Palestinian movement was growing, with the formation of the Palestine Liberation Organization, purporting to be political spokesman for all Palestinians, and many raids into Israel by Al Fatah, resistance fighters from Syria and Jordan.

The rapidly deepening crisis between Israel and her neighbors which exploded into the 1967 war was due to a number of complex factors: Israel's plans for diversion of the waters of the river Jordan, the problem of freedom of navigation in both the Suez Canal and the Gulf of Aqaba, the increasingly organized form of resistance of the Palestinians, and Israel's need to gain new markets.[19]

Border terrorist activities in Israel by Palestinian guerrilla bands from Syria and Jordan and military reprisals by Israelis mounted in fury. In October, 1966, several Israelis were killed by terrorists, and on November 13 an Israeli attack on the Jordanian town of Es Samu resulted in the death of eighteen Jordanian soldiers and civilians and the wounding of fifty-four more. Previously

191

King Hussein of Jordan had kept peace with Israel, but following the Es Samu incident he was almost overthrown because his people felt he had not defended them, and he thereupon joined Egypt and Syria in threats against Israel. On April 7, 1967, in an air battle near the Syrian capital of Damascus the Israelis shot down six Syrian planes.

As the Arabs came to believe that Israel was about to launch a serious attack on Syria, and as Nasser was chided by even moderate Arab leaders for his inaction in not defending Syria and Jordan, the Egyptian president secured the withdrawal of the U.N. emergency force from Egypt's border with Israel, sent military forces into the Sinai peninsula, and blockaded the Straits of Tiran, the entrance to the Israeli port of Elath. In accordance with Israel's warning of March, 1957, this last act was regarded by Israel as an act of aggression. Hence Israel's surprise strike in the hours just before dawn of June 5, 1967.

Though the June, 1967, war lasted for six days, it was practically won by Israel in only one day, for by that lightning predawn attack on June 5 Israel's air power wiped out the air forces of Egypt, Jordan, and Syria. Without support from the air, Arab ground troops were quickly defeated, so that by June 8 Israeli troops had occupied the Sinai Peninsula, the Gaza Strip, and all the Jordanian territory west of the Jordan River including the Old City of Jerusalem, and on June 10 the Israelis occupied the Golan Heights on the border of Syria. Thus after only six days Israel was controlling Arab territory amounting to more than three times the area of Israel itself.

Finally, on June 10, after demands by the U.N. Security Council, a cease-fire was arranged. But border fighting continued along the now blocked Suez Canal with heavy damage to the Egyptian cities of Ismailia, Port Said, and Suez, until a ninety-day cease-fire between Egypt and Israel was arranged in August, 1970. In the 1967 war France and the Soviet Union had sided with the Arabs, the United States with Israel. After the war both the Soviet Union and the United States poured vast military supplies into the Middle Eastern countries, and the area has remained a tinderbox ready to burst into flame at any moment.

The one major document which was hammered out after the 1967 war and which states the basic requirements for a peace settlement in the Middle East was the U.N. Security Council Resolution No. 242 adopted on November 22, 1967.[20] It emphasizes "the inadmissibility of the acquisition of territory by war and the need to work for a just and lasting peace in which every State in the area can live in security." The resolution also:

1. Affirms that the fulfillment of Charter principles requires the establishment of a just and lasting peace in the Middle East which should include the application of both the following principles:
    (i) Withdrawal of Israel armed forces from territories oc-cupied in the recent conflict;
    (ii) Termination of all claims or states of belligerency and respect for and acknowledgement of the sovereignty. territorial integrity and political independence of every State in the area and their right to live in peace within secure and recognized boundaries free from threats or acts of force;
2. Affirms further the necessity
    (a) For guaranteeing freedom of navigation through interna-tional waterways in the area;
    (b) For achieving a just settlement of the refugee problem;
    (c) For guaranteeing the territorial inviolability and political

independence of every State in the area, through measures
including the establishment of demilitarized zones.

Although both Israel and the Arabs have presumably
acknowledged the basic soundness of this resolution,
each has interpreted its provisions so differently that very
little progress has been made. Peace talks conducted by
U.N.-appointed Gunnar Jarring of Sweden accomplished
very little, for Israel at first refused to give up any
territory, and the Arab countries refused to discuss peace
with Israel. And both sides have continued to raid, and to
build up arms supplies with the support of the United
States and the Soviet Union respectively.

One interpreter of the Middle East summarized the
effect of the Arab-Israeli War in 1967 as follows:

In the wake of the June 1967 war between Israel and the
adjacent Arab states, two highly significant facts of the Middle
East situation became obvious. The first was the complete and
unquestioned primacy of Israel as the dominant power in the
region; the second was the emergence of the Palestinians as a
decisive challenge to the existing power relationship in the
area.[21]

In the years since 1967 Israel has occasionally indicated
willingness to give up some occupied Arab territory, in
part because of the problem of dealing with thousands
more Arabs within her boundaries. However, the rapid
establishment of many Jewish colonies encircling
Jerusalem and in what is technically occupied Jordan and
Syria has led many to conclude that, except perhaps for
certain portions of the Sinai Peninsula, Israel really has no
intention of ever giving back the land to the Arabs.

In June, 1967, Israel immediately annexed East
Jerusalem over the objections of many nations that this
action was a violation of the Geneva Convention of 1949.

Israel's announcement of her intention never to give up the Holy City is doubtless one reason for the judgment that "the annexation of the city of Jerusalem and the persistent attempt by the Israeli government to disfigure its cultural uniqueness may turn out to be the single most significant and potentially explosive consequence of the June, 1967, confrontation." [22]

In view of the stunning and humiliating defeat of the Arab forces in the 1967 Arab-Israeli War, many Palestinian Arabs in Israel and Palestininan refugees outside the country abandoned hope that Arab or other states would ever help them regain their homeland. Hence there followed violent guerrilla activity on the part of young Palestinian commandos, including hijackings of commercial aircraft, which provoked repeated retaliatory strikes by Israeli air forces. In "Black September," 1970, full-scale civil war broke out between the Palestinian commando movement and the government of Jordan. King Hussein crushed the Palestinian movement at the cost of thousands of casualties, and this resulted in great embitterment against the king for his lack of sympathy toward the Palestinian Arab cause. In subsequent years as frustrated Arab disillusionment has increased, so has indiscriminate Arab terrorism against Israel and Israelis, and therefore continued massive retaliation by Israel, especially against Arab guerrilla bases in Lebanon, with considerable loss of life on both sides.

The fourth Arab-Israeli war broke out very suddenly on October 6, 1973. It has since been claimed that Israeli intelligence had failed to appreciate the seriousness of President Sadat of Egypt's pronouncements about "the year of decision" at hand as well as the Egyptian military buildup along the Suez Canal. The Egyptian surprise attack on Yom Kippur, the Jewish Day of Atonement, resulted in immediate thrusts into Israeli-held territory, some eight miles across the Suez Canal into the Sinai Peninsula, and from Syria to the heights of Mount Hermon. During nearly three weeks of fighting, and after bloody tank battles in the Sinai, Israeli forces drove a wedge west across the Suez Canal between the Egyptian armies, recaptured the Golan Heights from Syria, and drove to within some twenty-five miles of Damascus.

On October 22 a cease-fire proposed by the U.N. Security Council was officially accepted by Israel and Egypt, although some troop movements continued. At last, however, on November 11, at a ceremony in a tent on a dusty Cairo-Suez road, Israeli and Egyptian officers, meeting face to face, signed a six-point cease-fire agreement. It was the first time since the establishment of the state of Israel more than twenty-five years before that Arabs and Israelis had met in direct negotiations.

This October war apparently created a new phase in Arab-Israeli relations. The war had been costly to both sides. Arab casualties had been an estimated 18,000 plus some 2,000 Syrian civilians killed in Israeli air raids. But the proportion of Israeli casualties had been considerably higher: 1,854 killed, 4,800 wounded, and 450 missing, from a total population listed at 3,309,000, some 83 percent of whom are Jews.[23] Of the Arab states Egypt and Syria had been the chief participants in the war, but other Arab countries had sent money and arms. Jordan had avoided direct confrontation with Israel, but had sent troops to assist Syria. Lebanon had opened its border with Israel to Palestinian guerrillas, but earlier Israeli raids into Lebanon, even as far as Beirut, had diminished the effectiveness of such guerrilla movements.

196

The chief new factor resulting from the 1973 war was the restoring of Arab pride and self-respect, which had been completely lost in the previous debacle of 1967. This time, probably largely as a result of Russian technical training, the Arabs had fought skillfully and successfully with sophisticated weaponry, though they had finally been outmaneuvered by Israel's expert, close-knit military command. And now, even though other Arab countries loudly objected, Arab and Israeli negotiators actually met to discuss disengagement. Now, as part of a peace settlement, Egypt and Jordan—and finally even Syria—willingly recognized Israel, and agreed to participate in direct peace talks at Geneva.

As these words are being written—October, 1975—Egypt and Israel have concluded an agreement by which Israel is to withdraw from some strategic mountain passes and oil fields in the western Sinai Peninsula under the surveillance of United States observers, and there is talk that the Soviet Union will shortly assist in a negotiated settlement between Israel and Syria in the disputed Golan Heights region.

Let it be clear, however, that even though the present situation may offer a faint glimmer of hope, permanent peace and prosperity are nowhere in sight. Both the United States and the Soviet Union, despite a so-called détente, continue to pour into their respective Middle Eastern satellite states vast stores of military equipment which may well explode into a nuclear war. Israel, feeling lonely and abandoned by all former friendly allies except the United States, harassed by frequent Arab terrorist attacks and responding by retaliatory raids, faces continued internal struggles—galloping economic inflation, intolerable military expenditures, widespread disagreement over appropriate foreign policy and treatment of Arabs, and the "cultural gap" between the new majority of Oriental Jewish immigrants since 1949, many of them refugees from Arab countries, and the original and dominant European-born Jewish citizens. Some more remote Arab countries have a new-found weapon in the oil boycott, in the light of the international energy crisis, but the countries immediately surrounding Israel—Lebanon, Syria, Jordan, Egypt—are undergoing severe internal political and economic struggles exacerbated by the plight of thousands of Palestinian refugees within their borders.

The 1973 war created relatively few new Palestinian refugees in comparison to the more than 200,000 Arabs who fled from their homes as a result of the 1967 Arab-Israeli War, and the multitudes before that since 1948. The total number of Palestinian refugees has been estimated at over 1,700,000 at present. It must be pointed out that some 60 percent of the Palestinian refugees have found new homes and jobs and have been assimilated into the economy of the Arab countries surrounding Israel. But the other 40 percent—the poor, the sick, widows and orphans, wives and children of unskilled workers, farm families—remain crowded into sordid refugee camps. These—and their Arab sympathizers—are, by an ironic turn of fate, the new "Babylonian exiles." Like the Jews of the time of Jeremiah they long for the day when they too can return to their homeland.

In the period since the war of October, 1973, Arab terrorist raids into northern Israel have continued, especially from southern Lebanon, with many and devastating counterattacks by Israeli forces. One new factor in the situation has been the rising role of the Palestinians in

198

looking toward a possible peace settlement. Though considerable systematic deportation of leading Arabs from Jerusalem and the West Bank of the Jordan River has taken place since the 1967 occupation, and hence the local population has lost much of its Arab leadership, the often seriously divided Palestinian leadership outside Israel has begun to become somewhat effective. Notably on November 22, 1974, exactly seven years after the adoption of the basic resolution 242 referred to above, the United Nations approved two more important resolutions, one declaring that the Palestinian people have a right to national independence and sovereignty, the other granting the Palestine Liberation Organization permanent observer status in the U.N. General Assembly.

With the snail's pace to date in negotiating a settlement of the current Middle East conflicts, far more vexing problems remain: a real facing of the issues concerning both Jewish and Arab refugees, the role of the Palestinians in the proposed Geneva Arab-Israeli conference, the future status of the city of Jerusalem.

4. Attitudes Toward the Continuing Middle East Conflict

The description in this chapter of the events of the first three-quarters of this century is intended to illuminate present-day Arab and Israeli attitudes toward the Middle East situation. In summary, the worst fear of the Israelis is that, given the continued population explosion in the Arab countries, and their oil-rich backing, they may perpetrate a new holocaust, massacring millions of Jews in an attempt to drive Israel into the sea. The worst fear of the Arabs is that, in view of the successive *faits accomplis* already experienced—the partition of the former Arab homeland by the establishment of the Jewish state of Israel, the vast expansion of Israel in the 1967 war, the Jewish settlements planted in occupied Arab territory since 1967, the refusal to permit Arabs to return—Israel will continue to expand to the boundaries of the ancient kingdom of David and Solomon and thus drive the Arabs into the desert. More moderate voices on each side urge the victory of elements within Israel pushing for the withdrawal from lands taken in the 1967 war and equitable treatment of all inhabitants, and the willingness of the surrounding Arab countries to live in peaceful economic and political cooperation with an Israel which has secure boundaries.

But what are, and should be, Christian attitudes toward these complex Middle Eastern problems? Let us attempt to state two violently opposing views which in some measure are to be found in present-day Christian circles.

On the one hand, an extreme pro-Israel view would include some or all of the following: For centuries Christian tradition taught that because the Jews were responsible for the death of Jesus and rejected him, they have been destined to be homeless wanderers on the earth. Hence Christians have been markedly unconcerned over such tragedies as Hitler's massacre of six million Jews in the holocaust. At long last, however, Christians realize the falseness of their former doctrine about the Jews, so that now they can and should repent and repay their centuries-long debt by total support of the Jewish homeland, the state of Israel. Indeed, any negative criticism of what present-day Israel does is really conscious or possibly unconscious anti-Semitism. Arab attacks on Israelis are an intolerable burden on the one respectable democratic state in the area. Furthermore, the Bible states that God gave this land to the children of Abraham, Isaac, and Jacob. Whereas the Crusades failed to rescue the land from the infidel, now providentially Jerusalem is once more the city of David's descendants.[24] Christians should therefore rejoice both in Israel's amazing progress in making the desert to "blossom as the rose" and in the restoration of the Jews to their rightful God-given heritage.[25]

On the other hand, an extreme pro-Arab view might include something of the following: Israel is really a tragic, but obviously now ineradicable, mistake in human history. The descendants of Abraham's son Ishmael, the Arabs, occupied the land for some thirteen hundred years previous to this century. During recent decades some Arabs and Jews lived peaceably side by side in the land, but the inhumane treatment of Jews in Europe and the West has resulted in the usurpation of the land by Jewish refugees. Hence, suffering for the sins of the West, the Arabs have lost their homeland and have reaped untold misery as scattered refugees. The state of Israel is thus the intrusion into an Eastern environment of a westernized racist state in which only Jews can be first-class citizens. Besides the inevitable suffering of minority citizens in Israel because of heavy taxation, inflation, and economic and political discrimination, the deliberate tactics of an occupying police state include dynamiting Arab homes and villages where the presence of Arab dissidents is suspected but not proved, imprisonment of agitators without redress, and expulsion of Arab leaders on flimsy pretexts. Arab terrorism, both inside and outside Israel, is the frustrated reaction of "freedom fighters" trying to

201

regain their homes or at least to get a hearing in the outside world. Israeli military reprisals, especially those against Lebanon, have caused inexcusable suffering among innocent civilian populations. While perhaps the state of Israel may continue to exist, it should immediately give up occupied Arab territory taken in the 1967 war and should preferably become a bi-national state allowing equal civil rights to all peoples. In any case, a modern prophet Amos must arise to cry out for justice and righteousness within Israel and throughout the whole Middle East.[26]

The above attempt to state such extreme polarity in possible or actual present-day Christian views is for the purpose of sharpening the issues.[27] Obviously both cannot be completely right, even though there be truth in both positions. What, then, is the Christian to conclude? The intent of this book is not to give answers, but to provide background information for enlightened individual and group decisions about these crucial matters. One Christian interpreter has urged a "new start" in attempting to bring Christian thought to bear on present-day Middle East conflicts and includes the following suggestions:

A new start must be based on an unequivocal concession from the Arab side of the right of Israel to exist, and Israel too must come to see that it cannot survive by military counter-attack forever.... Concerned Christians ... must start by affirming the principle of the interdependency of ... two causes (the development of new conditions for the Palestinians' existence and a commitment to Israel's secure survival)....

In the prophetic tradition divine donation cannot simply be translated into a secular land claim. Israel can be called the Zion of God only by those willing to accept the implication of this faith: Israel is not called to be a nation like other nations but must strive for the higher ethic of love and justice that will make it a beacon light of redeemed human relations *for all nations.* Therefore, a secular Zionism that appeals to the religious tradition of the Promised Land to make a secular land claim for the right of a state to exist "like other nations" turns biblical language into idolatry.[28]

This last statement referring to present-day Israel as in any sense the fulfillment of messianic prophecy reminds one of a famous New Testament incident. On that first Palm Sunday Jesus was riding on the colt down the Mount of Olives toward the Holy City. His loudly rejoicing disciples surely, but mistakenly, were expecting that once he entered the city, he would overthrow the Romans and establish his earthly messianic rule. But "when he drew near and saw the city he wept over it, saying, 'Would that even today you knew the things that make for peace! But now they are hid from your eyes'" (Luke 19:41-42). Did Jesus anticipate that Jerusalem, holy city to his ancestors and his contemporaries, the Jews, would become equally sacred to his followers, the Christians, and to the people of a faith which regarded itself as successor to both—the Muslims?

Notes

1. The text of this document, as well as much other valuable information in this chapter, is taken from the excellent World Studies Series volume, primarily a collection of firsthand documentary source materials, by C. H. Dodd and M. E. Sales, *Israel and the Arab World* (New York: Barnes & Noble, 1970), p. 63.
2. Maxime Rodinson, *Israel and the Arabs,* trans. Michael Perl (Harmondsworth, Middlesex: Penguin Books, 1968), p. 20.
3. Note, for example, Harvey Arden's article on Brooklyn's

Hasidic Jews, "The Pious Ones," *National Geographic*, 148, no. 2 (August, 1975), pp. 276-98, especially p. 289. Note also Gray, *History of Jerusalem*, p. 298.

4. Quoted in Gray, *History of Jerusalem*, p. 289.
5. While obviously the parallels are far from exact, note the somewhat similar assumptions when the ancient Israelites conquered the land of Canaan, and when the European colonists and later United States citizens took the land of the American Indian.
6. So Rodinson, *Israel and the Arabs*, p. 26.
7. So Gray, *History of Jerusalem*, p. 299.
8. So Rodinson, *Israel and the Arabs*, p. 32.
9. David Waines, *The Unholy War: Israel and Palestine 1897–1971* (Wilmette, Ill.: Medina University Press International, 1971), pp. 94-95.
10. For a summation of these competing claims to Palestine consult *Search for Peace in the Middle East*, rev. ed., a report prepared for the American Friends Service Committee (New York: Hill & Wang, 1970), pp. 18-22.
11. Dodd and Sales, *Israel and the Arab World*, pp. 74-76.
12. So Waines, *The Unholy War*, p. 102. Consult Richard P. Stevens, *American Zionism and U.S. Foreign Policy, 1942–1947* (New York: Pageant Press, 1962).
13. Dodd and Sales, *Israel and the Arab World*, pp. 78-82.
14. These statistics are taken from Alexander Melamid and Ellis Rivkin, "Israel," *The World Book Encyclopedia* (Chicago: Field Enterprises Educational Corporation, 1972), vol. 10, pp. 388-93.
15. These statistics are from Philip S. Bernstein, "Jews," *World Book Encyclopedia*, vol. 11, pp. 98-103.
16. *Israeli* is a modern term referring only to a citizen or inhabitant of the modern state of Israel. It should be carefully distinguished from the older term *Israelite*, which refers to a descendant of Jacob or a person belonging to ancient Israel. This important distinction is occasionally blurred—e.g., in a modern translation, or acknowledged paraphrase, of the Bible called *The Living Bible*.
17. Dodd and Sales, *Israel and the Arab World*, pp. 84-90.
18. *Ibid.*, p. 131.

19. Ibrahim Abu-Lughod, ed., *The Arab-Israeli Confrontation of 1967: An Arab Perspective* (Evanston: Northwestern University Press, 1970), pp. 87-88.
20. Dodd and Sales, *Israel and the Arab World*, pp. 182-83.
21. Ibrahim Abu-Lughod, "Altered realities: the Palestinians since 1967," *International Journal* (Toronto: Canadian Institute of International Affairs), 28, no. 4 (Autumn, 1973), p. 648.
22. Abu-Lughod, ed., *The Arab-Israeli Confrontation of 1967*, p. xi.
23. These statistics are taken from articles by Jay Bushinsky and William Spencer in *The 1974 World Book Year Book* (Chicago: Field Enterprises Educational Corporation, 1974), pp. 400-404.
24. In the summer of 1968, the year after the Arab-Israeli War, while visiting in an Arab home near Jerusalem the writer was shown a mimeographed document originating from an ultraconservative Christian group in the Midwestern United States which announced that already Indiana Bedford limestone was being readied and funds raised to rebuild the temple of Solomon in Jerusalem, so that the second coming of Jesus might be facilitated!
25. An example of a strong pro-Israel treatment is Christian E. Hauer, Jr., *Crisis and Conscience in the Middle East* (Chicago: Quadrangle Books, 1970).
26. An example of a strong pro-Arab treatment is A. C. Forrest, *The Unholy Land* (Old Greenwich, Conn.: Devin-Adair, 1972).
27. For a recent attempt at a balanced analysis supported by grants from the Charles F. Kettering Foundation, the Lilly Endowment, and the Rockefeller Foundation see Indar Jit Rikhye and John Volkmar, *The Middle East and the New Realism* (New York: International Peace Academy, 1975).
28. These suggestions come from an article by Rosemary Ruether, who in September, 1976, became Georgia Harkness Professor of Applied Theology at Garrett-Evangelical Theological Seminary, "Anti-Semitism and the State of Israel: Some Principles for Christians," *Christianity and Crisis*, 33, no. 20 (November 26, 1973), pp. 240-44.

The following are the resolutions on the Middle East and Jerusalem adopted by the Fifth Assembly of the World Council of Churches at Nairobi, Kenya, on December 9, 1975:

Resolution on the Middle East

1. The World Council of Churches has expressed concern regarding the situation in the Middle East on previous occasions. Events which have occurred in the area during the meeting of the Fifth Assembly in Nairobi have demonstrated anew that tensions persist there unabated.

2. We are concerned at the continued escalation of military power in the area which can only aggravate the threat to world peace from the unresolved conflict and stress the necessity for the great world powers to cease furnishing arms that maintain and aggravate tension.

3. We recognize that an international consensus has emerged as the basis for peaceful settlement on the following:

a) Withdrawal by Israel from territories occupied in 1967.

b) The right of all states including Israel and the Arab states to live in peace within secure and recognized boundaries.

c) The implementation of the rights of the Palestinian people to self-determination.

We are encouraged that the parties to the conflict seem to be progressively willing to accept these principles.

4. We recognize the Second Sinai Disengagement Agreement as a means of reducing tension between Egypt and Israel. However, since it is not addressed to the fears and distrust among Israel, other neighbouring states, and the Palestinian people, this Agreement must be followed soon by resumption of the Geneva Peace Conference for reaching a total settlement on the basis of the principles mentioned above. The Geneva Conference should necessarily involve all parties concerned, including the Palestinians.

5. We note that some Arab states have recently declared their readiness, with the participation of the Palestine Liberation Organization, to seek agreement with Israel based upon these principles.

6. Although the parties have not trusted one another suffi-
ciently until now to engage in dialogue, full mutual recognition
by the parties must be seen not as a precondition to, but rather as
a product of the negotiation. We call upon all parties to take
those steps essential to negotiations with hope for success.
Among these steps, we emphasize the cessation of all military
activity, both regular and irregular, including terrorism.

7. Peace in the Middle East must be based upon justice and
security for all concerned. The well-being of each party depends
upon the well-being of all other parties. We urge the churches to
help their constituencies to have more accurate information on
and more sensitive awareness of the various dimensions of the
Middle East conflict. The churches could thus help to promote
mutual trust among the parties and to develop a responsible
involvement in peaceful solution on the part of their members
and the governments of their countries. This opportunity is open
to churches within the area and the churches outside the area as
well.

Resolution on Jerusalem

1. For many millions of Christians throughout the world, as
well as for the adherents of the two great sister monotheistic
religions, namely Judaism and Islam, Jerusalem continues to be a
focus of deepest religious inspiration and attachment. It is
therefore their responsibility to cooperate in the creation of
conditions that will ensure that Jerusalem is a city open to the
adherents of all three religions, where they can meet and live
together. The tendency to minimize Jerusalem's importance for
any of these three religions should be avoided.

2. The special legislation regulating the relationship of the
Christian communities and the authorities, guaranteed by
international treaties (Paris 1856 and Berlin 1878) and the
League of Nations and known as the Status Quo of the Holy
Places, must be fully safeguarded and confirmed in any
agreement concerning Jerusalem. Christian Holy Places in
Jerusalem and neighbouring areas belong to the greatest extent
to member churches of the WCC. On the basis of the Status Quo

none of the church authorities of a given denomination could represent unilaterally and on behalf of all Christians the Christian point of view, each church authority of a given denomination representing only its own point of view.

3. Many member churches of the WCC are deeply concerned about the Christian Holy Places. However, the question of Jerusalem is not only a matter of protection of the Holy Places, it is organically linked with living faiths and communities of people in the Holy City. Therefore the General Assembly deems it essential that the Holy Shrines should not become mere monuments of visitation, but should serve as living places of worship integrated and responsive to Christian communities who continue to maintain their life and roots within the Holy City and for those who out of religious attachments want to visit them.

4. While recognizing the complexity and emotional implications of the issues surrounding the future status of Jerusalem, the General Assembly believes that such status has to be determined within the general context of the settlement of the Middle East conflict in its totality.

5. However, the Assembly thinks that apart from any politics, the whole settlement of the inter-religious problem of the Holy Places should take place under an international aegis and guarantee which ought to be respected by the parties concerned as well as the ruling authorities.

6. The General Assembly recommends that the above should be worked out with the most directly concerned member churches, as well as with the Roman Catholic Church. These issues should also become subjects for dialogue with Jewish and Muslim counterparts.

7. The Assembly expresses its profound hope and fervent prayers for the peace and welfare of the Holy City and all its inhabitants.